FROM SIDE-HUSTLE TO FREEDOM EMPIRE

FROM

SIDE-HUSTLE

TO

FREEDOM EMPIRE:

Chart Your Course to Passive Income with a Thriving Membership Site and Sail Away from the 9-5

By C.A. Walker and Elle McT

DIGITAL **BUSINESS**

42 BLACK

ISBN: 9798876102720
Imprint: Independently published

Disclaimers

FOR EDUCATIONAL AND INFORMATIONAL PURPOSES ONLY

This book is for informational purposes only and may contain errors. The authors and publisher do not guarantee the accuracy or completeness of the information provided. They are not liable for any loss or damage caused by the use of this e-book. The book provides educational resources but does not guarantee any specific results. Affiliate links may be included, but the book only affiliates with products and services that they believe will provide value to their customers. Any references to other products or services are not endorsements, and it is up to the user to conduct their own investigation.

EARNINGS DISCLAIMER

The authors warn that there is no guarantee of earning money through the techniques and ideas presented in their programs. Revenue and sales figures presented are exceptional results and do not reflect the average experience. The information provided should not be relied upon as a promise, guarantee, or expectation of success or earnings. Factors such as financial condition, experiences, skills, level of effort, education, and changes within the market will determine one's results. Running an online business carries risks and using any information contained on the website is at one's own risk. The content is provided without any express or implied warranties. The authors are not responsible for any decisions made regarding the information presented or as a result of purchasing their products or services.

NO WARRANTIES AND LIMITATION OF LIABILITY

The authors make no warranties regarding the performance or operation of their book and disclaims all warranties, including implied warranties of merchantability and fitness for a particular purpose. Users absolve the book of any liability or loss resulting from the use of this book or its resources, and the book is not liable for any damages incurred as a result of using this book.

Cover design by Elle McT

Printed in the United States of America

First printing edition 2024

www.42black.com

Dedication

This book is dedicated to everyone who has sat in an office, stood on their feet shift after shift, or watched the clock praying for the work day to end.

Table of Contents

Message in a Bottle

Ahoy there, mateys! Your digital buccaneer and ship captains of the "From Side Hustle to Freedom Empire: Chart Your Course to Passive Income with a Thriving Membership Site and Sail Away from the 9-5" here. Aye, that's a hefty title, but so's the treasure we're after: riches beyond a banker's wildest dreams... in the form of sweet, sweet passive income flowing freely from your very own membership website.

Now, if you're a salty sea dog, tired of swabbing the decks of the 9-5 grind and yearning for sun-kissed days on your own private beach, listen close! Forget landlubber guides – this ain't your grandma's dusty manual. This is a treasure map soaked in rum and sprinkled with pixie dust, leading you straight to a thriving membership empire built on your expertise and fueled by our sassy, no-nonsense guidance.

We've been sailing these digital waters for years, weathering tech squalls and battling SEO krakens, and boy, do we know the secret passages to passive income paradise. Whether you're a seasoned sailor in a new ocean or a landlocked dreamer with big waves of ambition, we'll be your trusty first mates, teaching you how to:

Chart Your Course: Pick your niche, build your pirate crew (aka audience), and raise the Jolly Roger of your brand.

Craft Your Irresistible Siren Song: Learn the magic of content that hooks 'em, reels 'em in, and keeps 'em paying month after month.

Tame The Tech Kraken: No techie jargon here, just clear instructions to steer your website like a seasoned captain.

Set Sail For Automated Profit: Discover the gold-filled islands of automation and passive income – no more swabbing decks for pennies!

So, ready to ditch the anchor of your boring job and set sail for freedom? Grab your copy of "From Side Hustle to Freedom Empire," and let's make your membership site dreams a swashbuckling reality! You'll be living the laptop-and- piña-colada life before you can say "shiver me timbers!"

Yarrr!

~ Captains of the Passive Income Fleet

P.S. Don't worry, landlubbers! We've also got a glossary for all the nautical jargon to keep you from walking the plank.

Introduction

The internet has revolutionized the way we communicate, work, and live our lives. It has opened up endless opportunities for businesses to expand their reach and connect with customers from all over the world. And with the rise of paid subscription models, companies are now able to monetize their knowledge and expertise.

Gone are the days when businesses could offer one-off products or services and still expect to thrive. In today's competitive landscape, it's all about delivering value and providing customers with a reason to pay for what they're receiving.

And that's where paid subscription websites come in. By offering exclusive content or services behind a paywall, businesses can cater to a niche audience and provide them with a sense of belonging. Paying subscribers get access to the best content without any annoying banner ads or other distractions, while businesses earn the revenue they need to keep their operations running.

Of course, not every website can succeed with this model. It takes a dynamic, comprehensive, and accurate site to cater to a niche market with information that nobody else has. But for those that do, the rewards can be immense. With a loyal following of paying subscribers, businesses can focus on delivering value and growing their brand, rather than worrying about generating ad revenue or chasing after uninterested visitors.

So, if you're looking to take your business to the next level and monetize your knowledge, a paid subscription website could be the perfect solution. And this guide has everything you need to get started, from planning and creating your site to launching, marketing, and monitoring it every step of the way. So why wait? Start building your paid subscription website today and take your business to new heights!

Unleashing Your Expertise: Who Can Thrive with a Membership Website?

The siren song of a thriving subscription website beckons to many, but who truly holds the key to unlocking its potential? The answer lies within anyone brimming with specialized knowledge, passion, and a desire to connect. Whether you're a seasoned expert or a passionate aficionado, if you possess unique insights and the drive to share them, a membership website could be your gateway to building a thriving community around your expertise.

Demystifying the Entry Point: The technical barrier to entry is surprisingly low. For about $10 a year, you can secure your .com domain name. Powerful website building tools, can cost as little as $25 a month, empowering you to craft your digital haven even with limited technical skills. Of course, professional designers can add flourish, but their fees might require deeper pockets. The choice is yours – DIY magic or polished expertise, both paths lead to your content kingdom.

The Golden Key to Expertise Unveiled: But wait, a magnificent website is just sets the stage. The true star of the show is your specialized knowledge. Think of it as a treasure chest overflowing with information that's rare, valuable, and difficult to unearth elsewhere. This could be data-driven insights, exclusive teaching methods, or expert coaching that makes complex topics approachable. Remember, your content should be a beacon of knowledge and in constant evolution, keeping your audience engaged and coming back for more.

Fueling the Passion Engine: And then there's the fuel that ignites this content engine – your passion. When you choose a topic that sets your soul alight, it becomes infectious. Your members, united by a shared passion, become more than customers; they become a vibrant community. Your enthusiasm becomes their compass, your expertise their map, and your shared journey the ultimate reward.

So, if you possess a unique skill set, a wealth of knowledge, and an unyielding passion to share it, then the world of membership websites awaits. Embrace the potential, tailor your expertise, and build a community that thrives on your unique spark. Remember, the key lies not just in what you offer, but in the passion you ignite and the connections you forge. In this digital landscape, your expertise is your treasure, and a membership website is the perfect map to guide you and

Why Membership Websites are Poised for Explosive Growth

Forget the gold rush; the 21st century's most lucrative boomtown lies in the digital landscape, with a thriving sector at its heart: membership websites. While many industries grapple with uncertainty, the subscription model has become a juggernaut, reshaping how businesses interact with their audience and generating recurring revenue streams that traditional models can only dream of.

Numbers paint a vivid picture:

Exponential Growth: The global subscription economy is predicted to more than double in size by 2025, reaching a staggering $524 billion. This translates to a mind-boggling 11.6% growth rate per year, leaving other sectors in the dust.

Dominating the Digital Landscape: From software-as-a-service (SaaS) giants like Adobe and Zoom to streaming platforms like Netflix and Spotify, subscriptions are fueling the digital economy. It's not just tech giants though; niche players like MasterClass and Peloton are proving the model's power in diverse industries.

Shifting Consumer Preferences: Today's consumers, especially millennials and Gen Z, crave convenience, value, and personalized experiences. Subscriptions deliver on all fronts, offering hassle-free access to exclusive content, ongoing services, and a sense of community, all neatly bundled into a predictable monthly fee.

But it's not just about the numbers.

Here's why the subscription model is a game-changer:

Recurring Revenue: Unlike one-time purchases, subscriptions provide a predictable, recurring income stream. This financial stability allows for long-term planning, investment, and scaling your business with confidence.

Deeper Customer Engagement: Memberships foster stronger relationships with your audience. Regular interactions, exclusive content, and personalized experiences create a sense of community and loyalty, translating to lower churn rates and higher customer lifetime value.

Data-Driven Growth: The subscription model provides a wealth of customer data and insights. By analyzing usage patterns and engagement metrics, you can continuously optimize your content, tailor your offerings, and personalize the member experience, leading to higher satisfaction and retention.

Scalability and Automation: Building a membership website leverages the power of automation. From delivering content to managing payments, technology takes care of the heavy lifting, allowing you to scale your business without being limited by time or resources.

And let's not forget the specific advantages for creators and experts:

Monetizing your expertise: Membership websites allow you to turn your knowledge, skills, and passion into a sustainable income stream, building a thriving business around your unique value proposition.

Building a loyal community: Attract an engaged audience who value your insights and expertise, forging deeper connections and fostering a sense of belonging that traditional models often lack.

Creative freedom and control: Membership websites offer a platform to direct your own destiny, curate unique content, and experiment with new ideas without relying on external gatekeepers or platforms.

So, how does this apply to you?

Starting a membership website is not just a trendy option; it's a strategic move that positions you at the forefront of a booming sector. You have the expertise, the passion, and the audience. Now is the time to capitalize on the power of subscriptions and build a thriving business that offers value, fosters community, and delivers recurring revenue – a dream combination in today's digital landscape.

Remember, the subscription revolution is just beginning. Don't miss your chance to ride the wave and carve your own niche in this dynamic and lucrative sector.

This is just the tip of the iceberg. Here are some additional ways to explore the potential of your membership websites:

Analyze your niche and audience: Delve deeper into your area of expertise and identify specific pain points and needs that a membership website could address.

Craft a compelling value proposition: Create a unique and irresistible offer that differentiates you from the competition.

Develop a content strategy: From exclusive insights and actionable resources to interactive sessions and community forums, craft a content plan that keeps your members engaged and coming back for more.

Explore pricing models: Test different pricing options and find the perfect balance between attracting new members and maximizing your revenue potential.

The opportunities are endless. Building your membership website can unlock the door to a world of recurring revenue, engaged audiences, and sustainable success.

Are you ready to join the subscription revolution?

Remember, you have the power to turn your knowledge into a thriving business. Take the leap, and build something remarkable!

Unlock Secrets of Value and Engagements From The Top Membership Websites

In the era of digital empires, membership websites reign supreme, capturing the hearts and wallets of audiences with their curated content, exclusive communities, and the intoxicating power of recurring revenue. But navigating the vast landscape of thriving memberships can be overwhelming. Worry not, intrepid explorer, for within the top 5 membership websites lie the secrets to illuminate your path to digital success.

1. <u>MasterClass:</u>

The undisputed Yoda of the membership universe, MasterClass, offers bite-sized wisdom from iconic figures like Neil Gaiman, Gordon Ramsay, and Serena Williams. The genius lies in **leveraging**

celebrity power to deliver premium video lessons, **mastermind-style Q&A sessions**, and a **sense of exclusive access** to unparalleled expertise.

Example 1: "Creativity & Leadership" by Spike Lee: This MasterClass delves into the mind of a cinematic legend, offering aspiring filmmakers and leaders alike lessons on storytelling, social responsibility, and building impactful careers.

Example 2: "Writing" by Margaret Atwood: The queen of dystopian fiction shares her craft secrets, demystifying the writing process and offering invaluable insights on character development, world-building, and navigating the publishing landscape.

2. Skillshare:

The democratization of learning shines bright in Skillshare, where thousands of passionate creators offer **diverse, project-based** online courses on everything from hand lettering to social media marketing. Their success hinges on **empowering everyone to become a teacher and learner**, fostering a **vibrant community** of creatives, and offering affordable access to a vast learning library.

Example 1: "100 Days of UX Design" by Ben Awad: This Skillshare course is a practical bootcamp, guiding aspiring UX designers through the design process, portfolio building, and landing design jobs. Its interactive, project-based approach keeps students engaged and motivated.

Example 2: "Watercolor Illustration for Beginners" by Sarah Watts: This course breaks down watercolor painting into bite-sized lessons, making it accessible even to complete beginners. Sarah's infectious enthusiasm and supportive community build a sense of camaraderie and accomplishment.

3. Peloton:

Forget the dusty gym; Peloton brings the fitness revolution to your living room with **interactive spinning classes led by charismatic instructors**. Their secret weapon? **Technology that seamlessly blends physical exertion with virtual community**, creating a **high-energy experience** that motivates users to push their limits.

Example 1: "Power HIIT 45" by Jess Sims: This high-intensity interval training class gets your heart racing and endorphins pumping with a pulsating soundtrack and Jess's no-nonsense motivation. The leaderboard creates a competitive spirit, urging you to push past perceived limitations.

Example 2: "Scenic Rides" by Cody Rigsby: Take a virtual bike ride through stunning landscapes from California's coastline to Morocco's desert, led by Cody's infectious positivity and playful banter. These rides offer a scenic escape while keeping you engaged and burning calories.

4. Substack:

For wordsmiths and thinkers, Substack provides a platform to **monetize their written content**, building a direct relationship with their audience. Its strength lies in **empowering individual creators** with a **simple interface and flexible pricing models**, allowing them to **curate newsletters, podcasts, and even gated archives** for devoted readers.

Example 1: "The Coddling of the American Mind" by Greg Lukianoff: This Substack newsletter by the co-author of the bestselling book of the same name delves into complex cultural and educational issues with clear prose and insightful analysis, providing subscribers with a thought-provoking platform for discussion.

Example 2: "Tiny Buddha" by Lori Deschene: This daily dose of mindful wisdom offers short essays on personal growth, self-compassion, and navigating life's challenges. Lori's relatable voice and practical advice resonate with readers, creating a supportive community in the comments section.

5. Patreon:

The champion of creators and patrons alike, Patreon empowers individuals to **directly support artists, musicians, podcasters, and other creatives** through recurring subscriptions. Its genius lies in **fostering a sense of partnership**, allowing patrons to feel personally invested in the creator's journey and enjoy **exclusive content, early access, and behind-the-scenes glimpses**.

Example 1: "The Adventure Zone" by the McElroy Family: This hilarious Dungeons & Dragons podcast offers exclusive live shows, bonus episodes, and early access to content for devoted patrons, who feel like part of the extended McElroy family.

Example 2: "Amanda Palmer" by Amanda Palmer: This singer-songwriter's Patreon offers a window into her creative process, with exclusive song demos, live stream Q&A sessions, and even personalized handwritten letters for higher-tier patrons. Amanda fosters a loyal community, feeling more like a bandleader than just a performer, blurring the line between artist and friend.

These five titans of the membership realm exemplify the power of understanding your audience, delivering consistent value, and building robust communities. But the beauty of this landscape lies in its diversity. From niche fitness platforms like obé for dance cardio to language learning communities like Duolingo, the possibilities are endless.

So, where do you fit in?

The key lies in identifying your unique expertise, passion, and target audience. What can you offer that no one else can? How can you create a membership experience that resonates deeply with your ideal members? Can you provide exclusive content, personalized interaction, or a sense of belonging that transcends mere information exchange?

Once you have this clarity, you can start crafting your own membership empire. Choose the right platform, design compelling value propositions, and leverage various engagement tools to foster a thriving community. Remember, authenticity, consistent value, and a dedication to your audience are the pillars upon which membership success is built.

Don't be afraid to be bold, to experiment, and to evolve. The digital landscape is waiting for your unique voice, your passionate expertise, and your commitment to building something remarkable. With the right ingredients and a dash of digital alchemy, you too can carve your niche in the ever-expanding world of membership websites.

This journey doesn't have to be solo. I'm here to guide you every step of the way, helping you analyze your niche, refine your value proposition, and navigate the technical intricacies of launching and running a thriving membership website.

Together, let's break the mold and build a digital haven where your expertise meets your audience's needs, generating recurring revenue and fostering a community that thrives on shared passion and value. Are you ready to claim your spot in the membership revolution?

From Seed to Sequoia:
Building Your
Prolific Membership Site

Forget overnight stardom, the rise of a thriving membership site is a slow-burning saga, a deliberate dance between passion and strategy. Whether you're weaving online courses, tailoring personal coaching, or crafting ingenious software, the key to sustainable success lies in nurturing the soil, tending to the details, and watching your venture blossom into a lucrative haven for your tribe.

This is no cookie-cutter journey, mind you.

The Initial Spark

Stage 1: Your "It" Factor

The first stage is all about igniting the "It" factor. You need to discover the hidden gold within your niche, the nugget so irresistible that folks will scramble to join your club. Marie Forleo's B-School, for instance, isn't just another business course; it's a meticulously crafted sanctuary for aspiring entrepreneurs, a perfect fit for its dedicated audience.

So, delve deep into the minds of your target market. What are their deepest desires, their nagging anxieties? How can your membership site be the balm, the compass, the secret weapon they desperately need? And is your pricing a bridge they can comfortably cross or an insurmountable chasm? Mastering this stage means unearthing the soul of your offering, ensuring it's more than just another "me too" in the digital landscape.

Stage 2: Sculpting

Now, Stage 2 is about sculpting the perfect model. Forget throwing together video courses and hoping for magic. Your content delivery needs to be a symphony, each element resonating with your audience's rhythm. Do they crave immersive live sessions? Bite-sized challenges that keep them buzzing? A treasure trove of downloadable resources? Choose the right delivery cadence, the sweet spot where engagement thrives and learning truly takes flight.

But a membership site isn't just a content dispenser; it's a vibrant ecosystem.

Stage 3: Art of Community

Enter Stage 3, the art of forging a real community. Your members crave connection, a sense of belonging that transcends mere access to content. Foster lively discussions, host interactive sessions, nurture a virtual campfire where stories flicker and shared experiences bind them together. Remember, engaged members become your cheerleaders, their enthusiasm attracting friends and fueling natural growth.

This is just the prologue to your membership site's epic tale. With each stage, you'll encounter challenges, witness unexpected twists, and celebrate milestones that solidify your success. But with dedication, a keen understanding of your audience, and a dash of creative enchantment, you'll watch your dream bloom into a flourishing community, a source of recurring revenue and joy for both you and your devoted tribe.

So, adventurer, are you ready to plant the seeds and embark on this rewarding journey? The digital landscape awaits your unique vision, your passionate expertise, and your commitment to building a haven where learning and belonging intertwine. Go forth, plant your flag, and cultivate the membership site that will stand tall and verdant for years to come.

Estimated Startup Costs

Basic Equipment: A reliable computer and desk to set up your headquarters – think $300-$1500 for the tech and $50-$150 for a comfortable workspace.

Incorporation: Legitimize your venture – a small price to pay for big peace of mind to protect your personal assets.

Domain Name: Your digital address! Secure your domain for about $6-1,000 per year depending on the top-level domain you choose (.com vs .inc).

Software and Plugins: This is where things get interesting. Research is key – some tools might be free, while others could hit the thousands. Don't skimp on the functions that operate the backbone of your site, but be smart and explore cost-effective options.

Security & Encryption: Trust is paramount! SSL certificates are a requirement. It shows your customers their data is safe and sound. Search engines also warn users if your site is not protected and it lowers your searchability. Most web hosts offer a free SSL certificate with Let's Encrypt. You can also invest in an SSL certificate like VeriSign's for around $300.

Design & Branding: If you're a design whiz, DIY your logo and website to save some cash. But sometimes, professional expertise (ranging from $150-$15,000) can be worth the investment to create a brand that truly resonates.

The key takeaway is to be informed, plan strategically, and optimize your spending – making every dollar work its magic to fuel your subscription dream.

Beyond the Launchpad: Scaling Your Membership Site to New Heights

Stage 4: Steady Growth

Ah, the initial launch buzz has dimmed, the email list skimmed clean. Yet, true success lies not in that ephemeral rush, but in the intentional, persistent pursuit of growth. Your launch was the ignition, now it's time to stoke the flames.

Offer a substantial free course, a honey trap, that leads eager minds to your paid haven. Videos, audio, written treasures – weave a tapestry of knowledge, a taste of the bounty awaiting them within. Build intrigue, kindle anticipation, and watch as they gravitate towards the rich buffet of your membership site.

Remember, list-building is a relentless quest, not a one-and-done feat. Nurture it, feed it fresh content, and it will become your ever-flowing spring of potential members.

<u>Stage 5: Tech Troubles and Triumphs</u>

Now, imagine your membership site at its zenith. Engaged members, a steady stream of new faces, your site hums like a well-oiled machine. But beneath the surface, an insidious foe lurks: clunky, duct-taped tech. Those cheap solutions that helped you bootstrap, they crumble under the weight of success. Everything needs custom coding, a frustrating, expensive labyrinth.

Fear not, weary adventurer! This is a hurdle many successful sites have faced. The answer? Ditch the fragile tech, embrace scalable solutions. Invest in plugins built for growth, boasting clean code, unlimited courses, and seamless CRM integration. Deep in the depths of fixing the underlying issues, off in the distance, like a beacon, your desire to clean it up for the promise land guides you towards automation paradise.

But functionality is just half the tale. Automation, that dream word for every time-strapped entrepreneur, is within your grasp. Upgrade your tech arsenal, from membership plugins to email marketing systems, and watch as manual tasks melt away. Your platform will hum with the magic of automation, freeing you to focus on what truly matters – your tribe.

And for those passionate about crafting their own unique teaching ecosystem. Build your platform, tailor it to your style, and let your voice ring out across your digital kingdom.

Is your site built for the sky, or tethered to the ground by its tech? Even if you haven't reached this stage yet, a proactive stance is key. A site thriving with 400 members deserves a foundation ready for 4,000. Act now, and avoid the upgrade headache down the line.

<u>Stage 6</u>: <u>The</u> <u>Art</u> <u>of</u> <u>Sticking</u> Power

Statistics like six-month lifespans may send shivers down your spine, but fear not! Retention is a battle every successful site fights and wins. Your weapons? Data, strategy, and a dash of member delight.

Analyze your reporting dashboard, uncover the metrics that hold the key to longer tenures. Is it fresh content, a la Carrie Green's monthly training courses in the Female Entrepreneur Association? Or perhaps a thriving community, woven from experienced leaders guiding eager newcomers? Gamification, too, can be a potent elixir, tweaking your courses and site to keep engagement bubbling.

And sometimes, a bold move is all it takes. Take Yaro Starak, masterminding his Blog Mastermind program. He recognized a three-month churn, a sense of endlessness weighing on his members. His solution? A six-month cap. The result? Retention doubled, income soaring in tandem.

Remember, your membership site is a living, breathing entity. It craves constant nurturing, strategic tweaks, and a passionate embrace of its potential. With each stage conquered, you'll witness its rise, a majestic testament to your vision, your dedication, and your unwavering commitment to your tribe. So, embark on this thrilling journey, scale the heights, and watch your membership site blossom into a haven where learning and belonging intertwine for years to come.

The Celestial Ascent - Where Revenue Reaches for the Stars

Stage 7: Summit of success

You've navigated the treacherous terrain of the previous stages, honed your site to razor-sharpness, and now – profit explodes like a supernova. Your members orbit your offerings, captivated by the gravitational pull of your brilliance.

No longer do you need to push or entice. Smart personalization ensures your content and offers resonate with each individual soul, like constellations tailor-made for their night sky. Interactive dashboards become portals to their progress, where achievements sparkle and goals wink enticingly. And strategized funnels, meticulously mapped like astrological charts, guide them seamlessly towards the next delectable morsel you've prepared.

This, my friend, is where loyalty thrives. Your members aren't just subscribers; they're ardent fans, eagerly awaiting your next celestial offering. They devour your courses, inhale your webinars, and beg to unlock the secrets hidden within your exclusive vaults.

But amidst this joyous explosion, remember this: the embers of growth must be stoked anew. Plan an organic, automated pathway, a cosmic ladder leading your tribe from product to product, each step igniting further excitement. Ensure your site can handle the celestial influx, scaling profitably without succumbing to gravitational collapse.

Prepare to Waltz

This journey, however, is not a single-shot linear ascent. Prepare to waltz through these stages, a cosmic dance. You might revisit Stage 3 to deepen community bonds, or Stage 5 to upgrade your tech as your orbit expands. Equip your team with the training to navigate the cosmos, and keep your own thirst for knowledge quenched.

Finally, dear adventurer, embrace the gift of automation. Let your systems hum with celestial efficiency, freeing you to step outside and savor the fruits of your labor. Watch the sunset paint the sky, knowing your digital haven thrives even in your absence. For life, like the universe itself, is vast and deserves to be explored with open eyes and a grateful heart.

So, go forth, intrepid entrepreneur! Scale the heights, reach for the celestial profits, and remember, even the brightest stars began as mere specks of curiosity.

Ahoy, Adventurers! Navigating the Shifting Sands of Membership Sites

Hoist the Jolly Roger, fellow captains! The tides of the digital seas are changing, and membership sites, once uncharted islands, are now thriving archipelagos brimming with opportunity. But like any seasoned buccaneer knows, staying afloat requires constant vigilance and adaptation. This chapter equips you with the keenest spyglass, revealing the emerging trends in the membership site industry – knowledge that will guide you in exploiting exciting opportunities and weathering potential storms. So, buckle your swashbuckling belts and prepare to dive into the exciting landscape of digital communities!

Charting the Course:
Rising Tides of Innovation

The winds of change are blowing, propelling new trends that reshape the membership site landscape:

Hyper-personalization: Prepare for a tidal wave of personalized experiences! AI and data analysis will craft bespoke journeys for each member, tailoring content, recommendations, and engagement strategies to individual needs and preferences. Remember, your crew wants to feel seen and valued, not just another deckhand in a faceless horde.

Micro-communities and Niche Power: Big isn't always better! Smaller, hyper-focused communities built around specific interests or identities are gaining traction. Hone your focus, captain, and carve out a unique niche where you can truly speak to the hearts and minds of your targeted crew.

Content Tsunami: Brace yourself for an overwhelming ocean of content! Videos, podcasts, interactive modules, and live events will vie for your crew's attention. Diversify your offerings, curate with quality, and remember, it's not just about quantity, but about creating immersive experiences that resonate with your niche.

Community-Powered Growth: Your crew aren't just passengers; they're the wind in your sails! Leverage member referrals, testimonials, and collaborative content creation to fuel organic growth. Remember, a community that feels involved and empowered becomes your most loyal and vocal advocate.

Navigating the Reefs: Obstacles and Challenges to Avoid

No voyage is smooth sailing, and savvy captains anticipate hidden reefs:

Content Fatigue and Attention Overload: With so much content vying for attention, keeping your crew engaged can be a battle. Focus on quality over quantity, prioritize interactive elements, and offer breaks from the relentless torrent of information. Remember, even the most engaging sea chantey loses its charm after endless repetition.

Data Privacy and Security Squalls: In these turbulent waters, data privacy is paramount. Be transparent about data collection and usage, implement robust security measures, and remember, trust is your most valuable treasure – guard it fiercely.

Burnout and Churn Storms: Keeping your crew happy and engaged is a constant quest. Stay in front of the storm by addressing fatigue with innovative strategies, encourage breaks and self-care, and remember, a happy crew is a productive crew.

Technological Tsunamis: The digital landscape is constantly shifting. It's important to stay abreast of new technologies, adapt your platform and offerings accordingly, and remember, a captain who gets bogged down in antiquated practices risks getting washed overboard.

Seizing the Treasure:
Opportunities to Exploit and Conquer

With the right map and a bit of grit, these trends can be your buried treasure:

Monetization Diversification: Don't rely solely on subscription fees! Explore tiered memberships, exclusive product offerings, and partnerships with complementary businesses. Remember, multiple revenue streams make your ship less susceptible to economic storms.

Global Expansion: Set your sights beyond your own shores! Translate content, adapt offerings to different cultures, and leverage online tools to reach international audiences. Remember, the digital seas know no borders, and expanding your horizons can unearth untold riches.

Live and Interactive Experiences: Fire up the cannons of engagement! Live Q&A sessions, interactive workshops, and virtual events can deepen connections, keep your crew captivated, and create a truly participatory experience. Remember, a static website is a lonely island; liven things up and make your community a bustling port of activity.

Building a Brand That Floats: Your site isn't just a platform; it's a brand identity. Cultivate a distinct voice, develop a loyal following, and remember, in the crowded digital ocean, a strong brand is the beacon that attracts and captivates your ideal crew.

Anchoring in Success:
A Legacy of Innovation and Community

Remember, fellow captain, membership sites are more than just digital empires; they are communities, havens of knowledge, and platforms for transformation. By navigating the trends and challenges with foresight and flexibility, you can not only stay afloat but thrive in the ever-changing seas of the membership industry. Embrace innovation, prioritize your crew, and remember, a successful site is not just about profit; it's about the legacy you leave behind, the connections you forge, and the impact you make on the lives of your loyal adventurers.

So, raise your Jolly Roger high, captain! Chart your course with the compass of these emerging trends, navigate the reefs of potential hazards with skill and determination, and seize the untold riches that await you in the ever-shifting sands of the membership site frontier. Remember, the digital seas are yours to conquer, and within this vibrant archipelago, you have the power to build a community that not only survives, but thrives, leaving an indelible mark on the lives of your crew and the wider digital landscape.

Bon voyage, fellow captain! May your voyage be filled with discovery, your crew ever loyal, and your legacy forever etched in the annals of the digital age. Now set sail, with the wind in your sails and the spirit of adventure in your heart, and embark on a journey that promises boundless opportunities and untold treasures within the ever-evolving realm of membership sites!

Unlocking the Vault:
Advantages of Paid Content Treasures

Forget the fickle whims of ad clicks and embrace the steady riches of the paid content model. While free websites gamble on fleeting ad dollars, your membership site dances to the rhythm of recurring revenue, a melody as soothing as it is profitable. Let's delve into the advantages that make this model a shining beacon for discerning content creators:

A River of Recurring Revenue

Imagine a tranquil stream of income, gently replenishing your coffers each month. Subscriptions become your loyal knights, tirelessly bringing you tribute in predictable intervals. The longer they linger, the more they bring, rewarding you for nurturing their loyalty. Unlike the boom-and-bust of advertising, subscription fees offer a soothing peace of mind, allowing you to focus on what truly matters – crafting content that captivates.

Startup Costs That Feel Like Pocket Change

Launching a paid site feels like a light stroll through a meadow, not a perilous trek through a financial desert. Costs, like the ever-present companions on any journey, are surprisingly low.

Your trusty laptop, a sturdy desk, and a dash of administrative magic get you most of the way. Hosting and design expenses? Shared by both free and paid sites, mere tolls on the road to success. Software, the mighty steed needed to carry your content treasures? Often accessible for free or at manageable prices. Security and payment processing? A reasonable investment to unlock the vault of recurring revenue. Low startup costs mean low risks, but remember, adventurer, this path demands dedication, not a get-rich-quick sprint.

Profits Soaring Like Dragons

With a steady income stream and light startup baggage, your profit potential takes flight. Reach the break-even point with the grace of a seasoned acrobat, your content the dazzling spectacle that draws in the crowds. Imagine, a single $50 monthly subscription, multiplied by even a small, loyal band of 200 followers, and your coffers overflow with riches. Each new member adds a feather to your profit wings, allowing you to soar to unimagined heights. And as your tribe grows, the whispers of your success spread like wildfire, attracting even more treasure-seekers to your doorstep.

A Solo Adventure (If You Desire)

Unlike brick-and-mortar empires, your content kingdom needs no sprawling army of employees. You, the fearless explorer, can navigate the terrain with nimble grace.

Sure, if technical woes raise their ugly heads, a friendly webmaster or database wizard might be needed. But by and large, your website thrives on your solo spirit. This lean operation translates to even higher profit margins, a sweet reward for your self-reliance. No waiting for HR cycles, no payroll woes – just you and your passion, crafting an empire fueled by your vision.

Scales Like a Mythical Beast

The beauty of your digital domain? It stretches and adapts with breathtaking ease. Need to add new content? A few clicks and your library expands. Want to welcome a larger tribe? Your platform gracefully accommodates the influx. Unlike physical limitations, your website scales with your ambition, ready to handle even the most gargantuan membership base. Remember, however, to lay the foundation for scalability during development, lest your castle crumble under its own weight. The physical costs of growth may be minimal, but attracting new members might require additional investment.

A Tribe of Devoted Disciples

Free content attracts a fickle crowd, drawn by fleeting trends and momentary interest. Paid content, on the other hand, cultivates a devoted tribe. Those who invest their hard-earned dollars become true disciples, eager to soak up your wisdom and engage with your offerings. This targeted audience translates to higher retention rates, a loyal band of champions who sing your praises and return for more. They may be demanding, seeking value in every nugget of content, but their dedication is a priceless treasure, a testament to the quality you provide.

The Art of Cross-Selling Treasures

Remember those mythical dragons hoarding mountains of gold? Your website can become a similar haven, overflowing with opportunities to share your bounty. Cross-selling, the art of offering complementary treasures to your loyal tribe, becomes a potent tool in your arsenal. Imagine, directing your bookworms to exclusive webinars or enticing your course participants with downloadable worksheets. Each member becomes a potential gateway to other offerings, a chance to deepen their experience and strengthen your bond. Successful cross-selling isn't a forced march, but a dance of fulfilling needs and exceeding expectations. Watch your members' eyes light up as you unveil the perfect complement to their current journey, and witness your business flourish as loyalty and value intertwine.

So, adventurer, are you ready to unlock the vault of recurring revenue? The paid content model beckons, a path paved with its own set of challenges, but also brimming with immense potential. Embrace the dedication, hone your skills, and watch your content kingdom rise, a testament to your vision and the enduring power of quality.

Treasures Beyond Subscriptions

While recurring revenue may be your membership site's lifeblood, it's not the only vein pumping riches through your digital kingdom. Let's explore two further pathways to wealth: the glittering caverns of affiliate income and the boundless lands of global reach.

Weaving in Affiliate Gold

Imagine your site teeming not only with your own offerings, but also with carefully curated treasures from beyond your borders. That's the magic of affiliate programs. Partner with trusted providers and e-commerce sites, weaving their links into the tapestry of your content like threads of shimmering gold. For each visitor who clicks through and discovers their riches, a portion of the spoils finds its way to your coffers.

But remember, adventurer, not all gold glitters equally. Choose your partners wisely, ensuring their offerings not only entice your members but also enhance their journey. An affiliate link should never feel like a treacherous detour, but an invitation to an even grander treasure trove. Only when their visit delivers genuine value will the magic truly work.

Global Passport Included

Forget the limitations of brick-and-mortar empires. Your website boasts a passport to the world, a gateway to millions across continents and languages. Even if your content whispers in a single tongue, fear not! Translation services stand ready to unlock communication, transforming your words into vibrant tapestries for diverse audiences. Search engines, too, play their role, bridging the gaps with their magic wands of translation. Suddenly, your niche market blossoms into a global village, eager to hear your wisdom and claim your offerings.

No longer are you bound by time zones or physical borders. Your site hums with life 24/7, a beacon for weary travelers seeking information, education, or perhaps a simple nudge towards persuasion. This, my friend, is the unparalleled power of the web – your voice ringing out to a boundless audience, day and night.

Leveraging Your Inner Alchemist

But your treasures needn't come solely from external partnerships. Look within, adventurer, for the goldmines of your own expertise. Perhaps you're a research scientist with secrets tucked away in cryogenic metals, or a university professor with wisdom overflowing your lecture halls. Have you considered transmuting your "know-how" into digital riches?

Gather your training materials, organize your knowledge, and let them sing through your subscription site. This, dear alchemist, is the art of turning potential into profit. If your information is unique, a beacon amidst a sea of mediocrity, there will be those who yearn for its light and gladly pay for the privilege of basking in its warmth.

Let your vision expand beyond the boundaries of your site. Embrace the possibilities of affiliate partnerships and global audiences. Forge your own wealth from the very knowledge you possess. Remember, your digital kingdom is a boundless realm, brimming with untapped riches waiting to be discovered. The only limit is your own imagination.

The Forge of Your Fortune: Choosing Your Paid Content Idea

So, you've set your sights on the Paid Content Frontier, eager to carve your own empire from the fertile fields of premium offerings. But before you wield your pickaxe, there's a crucial quest to embark on: forging the perfect idea. For without a treasure worth seeking, your adventurers (aka, paying members) will soon lose their way.

Remember, the web is a bustling marketplace, a glittering bazaar overflowing with wares both wondrous and mundane. To truly stand out, your offering must possess sparkling uniqueness, a secret formula that draws seekers from far and wide. Forget the siren song of "sell anything and everything" – that path leads to dusty corners and forgotten stalls. Your focus, dear entrepreneur, lies in delivering value, forging content that sings to the soul of a specific tribe, content that whispers "this is for you, and only you."

The internet acts as your trusty steed, carrying your offerings to distant lands and diverse audiences. It offers convenience, choice, and that touch of personalized magic. But let us not mistake the road for the destination. The content, the information, the very essence of your venture – that, my friend, is yours to create. It must be born from your passions, your expertise, your unique perspective on the world.

This section serves as your guidebook, a map of territories where Paid Content has flourished. From software secrets and literary labyrinths to exotic escapes and thought-provoking journals, each category a beacon hinting at the possibilities. But remember, these are mere whispers, not rigid blueprints. Your true idea lies waiting within, a hidden gem yearning to be unearthed.

Fear not the giants of the market, for sometimes, the smallest, most dedicated artisans craft the most coveted treasures. Look to the niches, the underserved corners of the web where passionate voices can fill the echoing silence.

So, adventurer, let your imagination ignite! Explore the categories, ponder your own passions, and forge your unique blend of value and intrigue. This is the first, and perhaps most thrilling, step on your journey to Paid Content glory. For within you lies the spark that can set the web ablaze – all you need is the courage to fan the flames.

I await your triumphant return, eager to hear the tale of your chosen idea, the cornerstone of your digital kingdom.

Auction and Marketplaces

Online marketplaces like Ebay or Elance are examples of successful sites that offer convenience, lower transaction costs, simplicity, and a large community of buyers and sellers. Nurturing a marketplace of teachers and tutors to help students online is a good idea.

Ideas

- Creative marketplace: Connect skilled artists and designers with clients seeking custom illustrations, logos, or graphic design work.

- Language learning marketplace: Pair native speakers with students looking for personalized language tutoring sessions over video chat.

- Niche hobby marketplace: Facilitate the exchange of rare parts, vintage collectibles, or handmade crafts within a dedicated community.

Business Information

This category includes business news, finance and investment advice, business research, digital content used for business purposes, business tips, and other information about all kinds of businesses. It also has business listings, corporate information, market research, and industrial reports and statistics. Market researchers, consultants, sales, and marketing managers need information about market trends, market size, major players in their sector, and a lot of statistics. This information can be difficult to find, and it can consume enormous time.

If you are experienced in information research, you can compile information on specific business sectors and companies and provide them to members with your own analysis. Almost all the large consulting companies offer paid content through their site; some use their site to offer their specialized market research reports. Corporate information from the financial perspective is another sought after category. It is valuable for both investors and analysts. You can also include business information and case studies pertaining to different countries and government.

<u>Ideas</u>

- Market research reports: Offer in-depth analyses of specific industries, competitor profiles, and future growth trends tailored to specific niches like healthcare or sustainable technology.

- Investment insights: Provide expert commentary and portfolio recommendations for financial professionals or individual investors, focusing on emerging markets or alternative assets.

- C-suite leadership resources: Develop exclusive content like executive coaching guides, industry best practices, and networking opportunities for CEOs and senior management.

Community Sites and Directories

Portals and community sites that promote interaction and collaboration between select groups of members. A large number of these are subscription member-only sites. These sites can offer additional services to their members, such as selling sports gear or advertising products from suppliers. Community Directories include sites whose content is created largely by other site visitors, for example, Ancestry.com, IMDB.com, and Classmates.com.

<u>Ideas</u>

- Professional network: Create a subscription-based platform for connecting experienced professionals within a specific field, offering mentoring opportunities, job postings, and industry resources.

- Alumni community: Build a dedicated space for graduates of a particular university or educational program to share career advice, event updates, and alumni-owned business listings.

- Genealogy research network: Offer exclusive access to historical records, ancestry mapping tools, and expert consultations for individuals researching their family lineage.

Consumer Research

Consumer research websites provide links to consumer booklets from government and corporate customer service centers, consumer advocacy organizations, and TV consumer transcripts. These resources cover a variety of consumer topics, including consumer price index links, college and scholarship resources, and other general resources.

They help consumers make informed decisions when purchasing items like new appliances, jewelry, wine, toys, or long-distance services. Some sites focus on specific topics, such as everything related to cars, including information on car buying, wholesale price lists, car reviews, and crash test results. They may also provide information on consumer rights under state lemon laws, and car complaint histories. You may also find telephone directories, including reverse directories by address, phone number or email address, company backgrounders, and directories of lawyers, consumer agencies, and organizations.

Consumer research websites may also cover information about home improvements, repairs, contractors, and home buying. Additionally, they incorporate health information and consumer information about nutrition, tobacco lawsuits, and medical news. There are several subject areas to choose from. Many sites have been set up for product comparisons, including features as well as price comparisons. These sites provide access to actual consumer feedback and experience from other buyers. While some sites are free, there are fee-based services for specialized and tailor-made advice.

Ideas

- Gadget Guru: Offer in-depth product reviews, expert comparisons, and exclusive discounts on electronics, appliances, and other household goods.

- Foodie Finder: Provide curated restaurant recommendations, personalized tasting menus, and cooking classes led by renowned chefs, catering to specific dietary needs or cuisines.

- Travel Trek: Develop customized travel itineraries, insider tips, and local guides for specific regions or adventure activities, like off-the-beaten-path hiking trails or hidden cultural experiences.

Credit Help Websites

These sites offer consumer credit history records and related content, credit counseling, and tips, as well as credit consolidation services. They provide articles, guides, and tips for credit improvement.

Ideas

- Debt Doctor: Create personalized debt payoff plans, negotiate with creditors on members' behalf, and offer educational resources on budgeting, saving, and responsible credit usage.

- Score Booster: Build a subscription service based on credit repair strategies, legal guidance for dealing with credit bureaus, and access to financial experts for one-on-one credit coaching.

- Investing Academy: Develop exclusive content for aspiring investors, featuring beginner-friendly guides, stock market analyses, and access to a community of experienced traders for Q&A sessions and mentorship.

Dating and Personals

Personals and dating sites are by far the most popular and visited category on the Internet. These sites foster matchmaking and dating, and include personal classifieds, chat rooms, messenger tools, and cater to a global audience. Some popular sites include Match.com and friendfinder.com.

<u>Ideas</u>

- Niche Romance: Cater to specific dating demographics or interests, like connecting professionals over 50, outdoors enthusiasts seeking active partners, or gamers looking for fellow video game lovers.

- Love Coach: Offer personalized compatibility assessments, online coaching sessions for overcoming dating anxieties, and access to professional matchmakers for curated introductions.

- Relationship Reboot: Build a membership platform for established couples, featuring expert advice on communication, conflict resolution, and keeping the spark alive in long-term relationships.

Ebooks

Ebooks are self-contained executable files of HTML or PDFs, similar to physical books, that can contain any content such as advertisements or links. They can be created using ebook generators and are good for marketing purposes.

<u>Ideas</u>

- Interactive Learning Guides: Combine text, quizzes, and multimedia elements to create engaging ebooks on specific skills like mastering a new software program or creative writing techniques.

- Niche Fiction Adventures: Write serialized novellas or short stories focused on a specific genre or target audience, like historical romance for time travel enthusiasts or dark fantasy for young adults.

- Professional Playbooks: Offer downloadable guides with actionable strategies and templates for entrepreneurs, coaches, or consultants in your area of expertise.

Education

Online education, also known as e-learning, is a highly effective method of providing training. The range of subjects and topics is vast, and the internet is an excellent tool for delivering cost-effective training. One of the biggest advantages of e-learning is that students can learn anytime and anywhere.

For example, there are sites that provide online driving lessons. In many states, first-time traffic offenders can enroll in a course that offers driving lessons and a test. If they complete the course, they may receive a suspended sentence. This has led to the development of numerous sites that follow a prescribed course according to the laws of a particular state, offering an online course and test on safe driving. Such sites have a large clientele!

Ideas

- Micro-Skill Masterclass: Design bite-sized online courses focusing on specific skills like mastering a new software program, writing effective emails, or building presentations, catering to busy professionals and lifelong learners.

- Creative Bootcamp: Build a community for aspiring artists, writers, or musicians, offering live workshops, personalized feedback from industry professionals, and access to collaborative projects and challenges.

- Coding Conservatory: Develop a subscription service with interactive coding tutorials, personalized learning paths, and mentorship opportunities for aspiring programmers, game developers, and web designers.

Entertainment and Lifestyle

Entertainment and lifestyle websites include digital music and multimedia, humor, recipes, travel, digital nomading, and other content that is intended for amusement, leisure, and diversion. This is probably one of the most visited website categories.

<u>Ideas</u>

- Curated Travel Experiences: Develop exclusive itineraries, insider tips, and downloadable resources for unique travel destinations, catering to adventure seekers, Eco-conscious travelers, or families with young children.

- Culinary Connoisseur: Build a membership platform offering personalized meal plans, cooking tutorials led by renowned chefs, and access to a global community of food enthusiasts for recipe swaps and culinary conversations.

- Digital Wellness Retreat: Create a subscription service featuring guided meditations, online yoga classes, and access to mindfulness experts for personalized coaching and stress management techniques.

Fan Clubs

Celebrity fan clubs offer memberships at reasonable annual rates and provide information on the celebrity, photos, news, and memorabilia such as discounted tickets and gift articles.

Ideas

- Historical Society: Build a community for fans of a specific historical figure, author, or musician, offering exclusive access to archival documents, expert lectures, and behind-the-scenes insights.

- Gaming Mastermind: Develop a paid community for fans of a particular video game, featuring walkthroughs, competitive tournaments, and developer interviews, catering to both casual and hardcore players.

- Creative Collective: Gather artists, writers, or musicians around a shared passion project, providing exclusive collaboration opportunities, feedback sessions with industry professionals, and early access to upcoming releases.

Games

Online games are a huge market, especially for kids and teenagers. Many websites offer interactive online computer games, such as arcade, sports, adventure, trivia, and card games. You can purchase game packages at low rates from other vendors and install them on your website. You may also develop your own games, but this would be far more expensive and time-consuming. Multi-player games have gained popularity as they allow people from different parts of the world to log on and play against each other, rather than one player playing against the computer. Many websites offer monthly prizes and sweepstakes to its members as a marketing strategy.

Ideas

- Brain Training Blitz: Design a series of interactive puzzles, logic games, and memory challenges, offering personalized progress tracking and leaderboard competitions for mental exercise enthusiasts.

- Virtual Escape Room: Create immersive online escape room experiences with branching storylines, hidden clues, and real-time collaboration features, catering to groups of friends or team building exercises.

- Educational Adventure: Develop interactive learning games for children that combine educational concepts with engaging characters and playful storytelling, making learning fun and engaging.

Greeting Cards

Greeting card websites offer a great way to send wishes to loved ones all over the world. Electronic greetings are more convenient and cheaper than paper greetings. You can find online greeting cards for every occasion, from birthdays to weddings and festivals. They also include general love and friendship cards.

Electronic greetings are interactive and animated. Initially, most websites offered online greeting cards for free, but this trend has changed in recent years. Quality sites now offer paid subscriptions at nominal rates. Revenue generated in this category includes revenue from the attachment of gift certificates to content. BlueMountain and AmericanGreetings are two of the most popular greeting card websites.

Ideas

- Personalized Poetry Studio: Allow users to commission custom poems for special occasions, offering different styles and themes, with optional recording or video delivery for a unique touch.

- Charity Greeting Cards: Partner with non-profit organizations to create exclusive collections of digital greeting cards, where a portion of the proceeds go towards supporting their cause.

- Interactive Story Cards: Design animated and personalized greeting cards that tell heartwarming stories or unfold playful jokes, offering a more immersive and memorable experience than traditional cards.

Health and Fitness

Fitness and health, diets, and weight loss sites provide complete guides, articles, tips, and counseling on proper eating and exercising habits, benefits of diet and exercise, fitness techniques, diet articles and tips, weight loss, as well as some popular diet plans.

These sites may include tips from fitness experts, reviews of fitness and diet programs, message boards, forums, and discussions on health and fitness. They may also provide information on various nutritional and diet supplements and healthy and non-healthy foods. Some popular fitness and health sites are eDiets.com and WeightWatchers.com. Generally, such sites will also offer privileges and discounts to their members for fitness equipment, nutritional supplements, or memberships at fitness clubs.

Ideas

- Personalized Training Platform: Design a subscription service with workout plans tailored to individual fitness goals and preferences, featuring video exercises, progress tracking tools, and access to certified trainers for one-on-one coaching.

- Mindful Movement Studio: Offer online yoga and meditation classes focused on specific needs like stress reduction, pre-natal health, or injury recovery, led by experienced instructors with a holistic approach.

- Nutrition Academy: Build a membership community sharing delicious and healthy recipes, personalized meal plans based on dietary restrictions, and live Q&A sessions with registered dietitians and nutritionists.

Horoscope and Family Tree

These specialized sites offer to read and interpret individual and family horoscopes, as well as trace and maintain family trees with access to centuries of historical data. Members can include family photos, documents, and more on the site for their friends to view.

Ideas

- Cosmic Coaching: Develop personalized astrological readings focusing on career changes, relationship compatibility, or major life transitions, incorporating insights from birth charts and transiting planets.

- DNA Detective: Offer a subscription service for ancestry research, connecting users with historical records, genetic matching tools, and expert genealogists to help build their family trees and uncover fascinating stories.

- Legacy Builder: Create a platform for preserving family memories, sharing treasured photos, documents, and stories, allowing members to collaborate on building a digital archive for future generations.

Legal Research

Legal research websites are an effective resource for all kinds of legal information. They provide information on laws ranging from advertising, automobile, home buying, marketing, business, matrimonial, debt collection, education, criminal, computer security, constitutional, commercial, bankruptcy, to anti-terrorism.

You can find a list of attorneys for all states as well as a list of organizations and associations for legal issues. Information on bar associations, law schools, human rights services, and immigration services could also be incorporated. Case records may be annotated and indexed to offer powerful search and retrieval facilities. One of the best-known sites in this category is LexisNexis.

Ideas

- Compliance Corner: Offer subscription access to in-depth legal analyses and updates on specific industry regulations, relevant case studies, and practical guides for businesses to stay compliant and avoid legal risks.

- Litigation Prep Platform: Build a community for lawyers by providing access to expert witness directories, downloadable trial templates, and collaborative tools for case strategy and document sharing.

- Pro Se Powerhouse: Develop a subscription service with affordable legal forms, personalized guidance on navigating the court system, and access to resources like online legal dictionaries and self-help guides for individuals facing legal challenges.

Medical Research

Medical research websites focus on medical issues and health insurance. They provide an extensive list of research resources on various diseases and promote public education on health. These websites offer clinical information, details about doctors and hospitals in all states, information on medical ethics and fraud, medical journals, publications, articles, as well as information related to Medicare and health insurance.

These sites are a great resource for consultants, legal researchers, consumers, and anyone interested in National Institutes of Health, medical encyclopedias, and dictionaries. They also provide extensive information on prescription and nonprescription drugs.

You can consider a site that provides information on health and medicine for the general public or for a specific target group, such as women or nursing mothers. There is also considerable interest in alternative and complementary medicine and therapy.

Ideas

- Personalized Health Reports: Analyze users' genetic data and medical history to provide them with customized reports on disease risks, preventative measures, and recommended lifestyle changes.

- Chronic Disease Management Platform: Build a community for individuals with specific chronic conditions, offering access to expert Q&A sessions, support groups, and personalized guidance from healthcare professionals.

- Drug Discovery Hub: Create a subscription platform for early access to research papers, clinical trial updates, and expert commentary on the latest advancements in pharmaceutical development.

Newsletters

Newsletters are also a great way to develop a member base and should be educative and informative for a relevant customer base.

Ideas

- Niche Industry Insights: Tailor your newsletter to a specific industry, delivering curated news, expert analysis, and actionable advice for entrepreneurs, investors, or professionals in that field.

- Daily Digest for Busy Professionals: Compile a concise and informative digest of essential news, market trends, and industry updates relevant to working professionals, delivered straight to their inboxes each morning.

- Creative Inspiration Hub: Curate a weekly newsletter featuring inspiring stories, interviews with successful creatives, and exclusive tutorials or tips from artists, writers, or musicians.

People Search

People search websites are useful for finding addresses and other information on people, especially lost friends and relatives. Site owners purchase databases of public records from government and other agencies, making it easier to track people down. You could search for people by name, address, or phone number. Some people search websites also provide background checks for higher fees. Property and business searches may also be included.

<u>Ideas</u>

- Family History Detective: Offer genealogical research services, access to historical records archives, and expert guidance to help individuals trace their family lineage and uncover fascinating ancestral stories.

- Missing Persons Network: Build a platform for connecting families searching for missing loved ones with potential leads, volunteer resources, and expert advice on navigating the search process.

- Background Check Platform: Develop a subscription service for individuals or businesses seeking professional background checks on potential employees, business partners, or tenants, with varying levels of detail and affordability.

Self-Help and Advice

Personal advice, motivation, and self-help sites are aimed at individuals, offering tips, articles, advice, and counseling on how to build self-esteem, self-confidence and reduce stress for a happier life. These sites may also provide inspirational quotations, stories, poems, and other resources to motivate and inspire visitors. They could include psychology tests, IQ tests, emotional intelligence tests, and personality tests for self-improvement. Personal advice and counseling for students is a big market, and educational counseling can be provided through such sites. Professional advisory information and training is covered in a subsequent category.

Ideas

- Mental Fitness Bootcamp: Design a gamified self-help program with interactive exercises, mindfulness coaching, and personalized progress tracking to help users combat anxiety, depression, and build emotional resilience.

- Relationship Reboot Masterclass: Offer online workshops and coaching sessions led by relationship experts, focusing on conflict resolution, communication skills, and rebuilding trust for individuals or couples seeking to revitalize their relationships.

- Financial Freedom Roadmap: Develop a subscription service with financial planning tools, budget templates, and expert guides to help individuals achieve their financial goals, from debt repayment to building wealth and securing retirement.

Sports

Sports news and information websites feature the latest sports news from around the world, information on all kinds of sports, sporting personalities, and venues. They also offer chat rooms, message boards, and forums for sports fans to interact with each other. Such websites could provide links to various league sites and sell sporting goods and memorabilia to members.

<u>Ideas</u>

- Fantasy Sports Mastermind: Create a premium platform for fantasy sports enthusiasts, offering advanced data analysis tools, exclusive player projections, and access to a community of expert coaches for advice and strategy discussion.

- Athlete Training Academy: Build a subscription service for aspiring athletes, featuring online training programs tailored to specific sports, personalized video feedback from professional coaches, and access to sports psychologists and nutritionists.

- Global Sports Adventure: Develop a unique membership program offering exclusive access to behind-the-scenes experiences at major sporting events, cultural immersion in sports-centric countries, and opportunities to meet legendary athletes and coaches.

Technical Helpdesk and Advice Websites

Technical helpdesk websites offer a 24/7 computer helpdesk hotline with telephone support at a fixed cost for members. They provide assistance with installation, configuration, and system set-up for hardware, operating systems, and software applications.

Ideas

- Cybersecurity Concierge: Offer premium technical support specifically focused on cybersecurity, providing real-time threat monitoring, vulnerability assessments, and personalized guidance for individuals and businesses seeking advanced online protection.

- Gadget Guru Hotline: Build a subscription service for tech enthusiasts and early adopters, featuring priority access to expert troubleshooting support for new devices, software troubleshooting, and in-depth product reviews with comparative analyses.

- Senior Tech Savvy Club: Develop a community-driven platform for older adults, offering online workshops and live Q&A sessions on basic digital literacy skills, safe internet browsing, and utilizing technology to connect with family and friends.

Training

Online training is available for nursing, gardening, interior decoration, alternative medicine, personal growth, and development. Many such sites are increasing rapidly. Some teach people how to lose weight and remain fit, while others teach time management, leadership skills, or the cultures and languages of the world. Subscription websites have become a popular way for companies to provide training to their employees.

Online universities offer training on subjects such as HIPAA (the regulation that covers hospitals, medical providers, and health insurance companies, whereby training is required on the subject of maintaining security and privacy of medical records), computer programming, and other topics that are essential for businesses and their employees.

Test preparation training and practice is another area in which subscription or paid content websites excel. Students preparing for exams such as SAT, GRE, GMAT, LSAT, or those who aspire to obtain industry-recognized certifications such as MCSE (Microsoft Certified Systems Engineer) can sign up as members on these sites and receive practice tests and tips for their examinations.

Ideas

- Creative Skills Bootcamp: Design intensive online workshops focusing on specific creative skills like web design, video editing, or animation, featuring industry-vetted instructors, personalized feedback, and practical portfolio-building projects.

- Mindfulness Mastery Academy: Build a subscription platform with guided meditations, expert talks on mindfulness practices, and access to a global community for individuals seeking stress reduction, emotional well-being, and inner peace.

- Sustainable Living Masterclass: Develop a series of online modules on topics like organic gardening, renewable energy options, and eco-friendly home improvement, offering actionable steps and community support for individuals embracing greener lifestyles.

Remember, these are just starting points to inspire your specific niche within each category. Focus on your unique expertise, target underserved communities, and offer high-quality, personalized content to stand out in the crowd. With innovative ideas and valuable resources, you can build a thriving paid content business in any sector, helping your audience make informed decisions, improve their lives, and find connections they wouldn't have discovered elsewhere.

Five Thriving Business Ideas

Whether you're driven by a lifelong passion, a newly found skill, or the desire to share your wisdom, the entrepreneurial spirit within you yearns to take flight. But where to begin? The business landscape is vast, and choosing the right venture can feel daunting. Fear not, intrepid adventurer, for within this section you'll find five thriving business ideas ready to ignite your journey, each bursting with potential and primed for success.

1. Coaching and Consulting:

Your years of experience, honed skills, and accumulated wisdom are your most valuable assets. Leverage them to build a thriving coaching or consulting practice, guiding others towards their goals in diverse fields.

Life Coaching: Empower individuals to navigate life's transitions, overcome challenges, and achieve personal growth. Your insights and empathetic guidance can transform lives, building a loyal clientele eager for your wisdom.

Business Coaching: Aspiring entrepreneurs and seasoned professionals alike seek your expertise in strategic planning, marketing, and leadership. Help them build successful ventures and navigate the complexities of the business world.

Wellness Coaching: Share your knowledge of nutrition, fitness, and holistic living, guiding clients towards healthier, happier lives. Cater to specific niches like yoga coaching, nutrition coaching, or stress management, building a devoted community on their wellness journey.

Examples

Marie Forleo: This renowned life coach offers online courses, live events, and one-on-one coaching, empowering millions to build dream businesses and live authentic lives.

Kathyrn Minshew: Her "Honeycomb" platform connects experienced business leaders with women entrepreneurs, providing invaluable mentorship and guidance.

Rachaele Hamu: A leading figure in holistic health, Rachaele's "Live Light Global" offers personalized coaching and retreats, guiding individuals towards optimal well-being.

2. <u>E-commerce</u> <u>Stores:</u>

Unleash your inner curator and build an online haven for discerning shoppers. From handcrafted treasures to curated collections, the possibilities are endless.

Home Decor: Cater to the growing desire for unique and personalized living spaces. Offer handcrafted ceramics, vintage furniture finds, or sustainable homeware, transforming houses into homes.

Fashion Accessories: Tap into the ever-evolving fashion world with thoughtfully curated jewelry, scarves, or bags. Focus on niche markets like ethical fashion or artisanal craftsmanship, standing out from the crowd.

Health and Wellness: The demand for natural and organic products is booming. Sell herbal teas, essential oils, or handmade aromatherapy candles, catering to the holistic lifestyle trend.

<u>Examples</u>

Rifle Paper Co.: Anna Bond's online store is a dreamland of vibrant stationery, home goods, and accessories, infused with her distinctive floral patterns and whimsical touches.

The Dreslyn: Founded by two moms seeking chic yet comfortable clothing, The Dreslyn offers curated collections of ethically sourced apparel for the modern woman.

Moon Juice: Amanda Chantal Bacon's e-commerce empire offers adaptogenic blends, herbal supplements, and moon-phase-aligned wellness products, catering to the conscious consumer.

3. <u>Digital</u> <u>Product</u> <u>Creation:</u>

Share your knowledge and expertise with the world through digital products like online courses, ebooks, or printables.

Online Courses: Whether you're a culinary master, a creative writing guru, or a coding whiz, share your skills through engaging online courses. Platforms like Udemy and Skillshare make it easier than ever to reach a global audience.

Ebooks: Compile your insights on a specific topic or write a captivating fictional tale. With self-publishing platforms readily available, the power to become a published author rests in your hands.

Printables and Templates: Organize lives and boost productivity with beautifully designed planners, calendars, or budget trackers. The demand for practical yet aesthetically pleasing printables is ever-growing.

<u>Examples</u>

Lindsay Adler: This renowned writing coach has helped thousands develop their craft through her online courses and popular book, "Write With Confidence."

Shauna Niequist: The bestselling author, blogger, and speaker offers inspirational ebooks and audio courses on faith, motherhood, and living a meaningful life.

Emily Ley: Known for her vibrant planners and organizational tools, Emily Ley's digital products empower individuals to take control of their schedules and achieve their goals.

4. <u>Freelancing</u> and <u>Consulting:</u>

Unleash your professional skills and land remote gigs in diverse fields. From writing and editing to graphic design and social media management, the freelance world offers flexibility and limitless possibilities.

Content Writing: Websites, blogs, and social media platforms crave engaging content. Offer your writing expertise in specific niches like healthcare, technology, or travel, securing consistent freelance work.

Virtual Assistant: Provide administrative, technical, or creative support to busy professionals and entrepreneurs. From managing emails and schedules to designing graphics and managing social media, your virtual assistance skills can be your ticket to freedom and fulfillment.

Social Media Management: Businesses of all sizes need help navigating the ever-changing social media landscape. Offer your expertise in content creation, community management, and paid advertising, helping brands build a strong online presence.

Examples

Upwork: This platform connects freelancers with clients for a variety of projects, from writing and editing to web development and marketing.

Fiverr: Offering micro-services like logo design, social media posts, and data entry, Fiverr allows freelancers to monetize their skills in bite-sized tasks.

The Virtual Assistant Hub: This online community and resource center for virtual assistants provides training, networking opportunities, and job postings, empowering individuals to build successful freelance careers.

5. <u>Blogging</u> and <u>Influencer</u> <u>Marketing:</u>

Share your passions, expertise, and unique voice with the world through blogging and social media. Build a dedicated audience and leverage it to create diverse income streams.

Lifestyle Blogging: From fashion and beauty to travel and DIY, the world of lifestyle blogging offers endless possibilities. Share your curated content, experiences, and insights, attracting brands and creating opportunities for sponsored content and collaborations.

Niche Blogging: Become an authority in a specific field, whether it's gardening, personal finance, or pet care. Build a loyal following of engaged readers and monetize your blog through advertising, affiliate marketing, and even online courses.

Social Media Influencer: With the rise of Instagram and TikTok, influencers are changing the game. Share your expertise, personality, and creative content on these platforms, attracting brands and creating partnerships that leverage your influence.

<u>Examples</u>

Marie Kondo: This decluttering guru rose to fame through her blog and bestselling books, now building a global empire through consulting, online courses, and branded products.

Gary Vaynerchuk: From wine entrepreneur to social media expert, Gary Vaynerchuk's online presence is a force to be reckoned with. He advises businesses on social media strategy and has built a loyal following through his engaging content and actionable advice.

Chiara Ferragni: This Italian fashion blogger turned entrepreneur has parlayed her social media influence into a multi-million dollar fashion empire, proving the power of building a dedicated online community.

Remember, these are just a starting point. Your passions, skills, and unique voice are your strongest assets. Blend them with market trends, research your niche, and create a business that reflects your individuality and resonates with your ideal audience. The journey won't be easy, but with dedication, resilience, and a dash of passion, you can build a thriving venture that brings you joy and financial freedom.

So, embrace your inner explorer, choose your business adventure, and embark on a journey of entrepreneurial success. Remember, your age and experience isn't a finish line, it's a launching pad for your most daring dreams. Go forth and conquer!

Finding Your Content Niche:
A Compass for Success

Now that we've explored a wide range of captivating content ideas and compelling business models, it's time to chart your unique course. The secret sauce lies in pinpointing the idea that'll make your subscription website stand out from the crowd and set it on the path to success. So, grab your conceptual compass and let's navigate the key factors that'll guide you towards the perfect content niche:

1. Chart Your Expertise: The journey begins with introspection. What are you passionate about? What skills and knowledge do you possess that others value? Chances are, you already have expertise in something that could be woven into the fabric of a thriving subscription site. Look beyond your primary income source – think of hidden gems, like a knack for baking artisan bread or a mastery of historical trivia. Remember, your expertise is the foundation of your site's value proposition.

2. Define Your Value Map: Once you've identified your domain, delve deeper. What unique service do you offer (or plan to offer)? How do you deliver it differently from the competition? Why would someone value your approach? And where can you find your ideal audience? Jot down answers to these questions, mapping out your strengths and weaknesses. This strategic self-analysis will provide invaluable direction as you shape your content experience.

3. Know Your Strengths & Weaknesses: No expert is infallible. Own your strengths – what makes you stand out in the crowd? Perhaps it's your engaging writing style, your deep understanding of a niche topic, or your ability to translate complex concepts into actionable steps. But don't shy away from identifying your weaknesses too. Are there gaps in your knowledge that need filling? Areas where you could refine your delivery or enhance your platform's functionality? Acknowledging your weaknesses paves the way for continuous improvement and ensures your content remains sharp and relevant.

By considering these factors, you'll move beyond a sea of generic ideas and discover the unique space where your expertise sparks with your audience's needs. Remember, it's not just about what you offer, but how you offer it, and why it matters.

Finding Your Niche's North Star

The journey to a thriving subscription site takes a sharp turn here – towards understanding your ideal audience and carving out a space that's undeniably yours. Buckle up, because it's time to become a master navigator of your niche!

1. Sharpen Your Audience Focus: Every successful entrepreneur knows – you can't please everyone. That's why defining your target audience is like drawing a treasure map, leading you to the buried gold of satisfied subscribers. Craft a detailed profile of your ideal client, considering their age, gender, background, interests, and even income level. Think of it as painting a vibrant portrait of who you're creating for. Don't forget to map out who isn't your ideal prospect – this clarity helps focus your marketing efforts like a laser beam.

2. Unearthing the "Why?": Knowing your audience isn't enough; you need to understand their deepest desires and anxieties. How will your service solve their problems or fuel their passions? What questions keep them up at night? Answering these questions unveils the "why" behind your content, the emotional hook that draws them in and keeps them coming back for more. Remember, it's not just about what you offer, but the transformation you promise.

3. The Spark of Originality: In the bustling online marketplace, standing out is paramount. Your unique selling proposition (USP) is the crown jewel of your site, attracting subscribers like moths to a flame. Invest in originality – offer specialized information, content unavailable elsewhere, or a twist on familiar offerings. Remember, copycats fade fast, while innovators blaze trails.

4. Beyond Uniqueness - Enter The Value Vault: Even the most original spark needs nurturing. Consider value-added extras like steeper discounts, exclusive communities, or personalized services. Think of it as building a treasure chest of benefits that keeps your audience coming back for more, even when competitors beckon. Offbeat offerings, unique perspectives, and dependable reliability can also be your secret weapons in the battle for subscriber loyalty.

5. Know Your Neighbors: Competition? More Like Inspiration! While uniqueness is key, studying your competitors is like having a secret map to hidden pitfalls and shortcuts. Analyze their strengths and weaknesses, dissect customer reviews, and discover untapped needs. Use this intel to carve out your own niche, filling gaps your rivals leave behind. Sometimes, even if a market looks saturated, your fresh approach can be the key that unlocks a new wave of loyal subscribers.

6. Resource Check - Fueling Your Content Engine: You've unearthed a brilliant idea, crafted a niche, and identified your tribe. Now, it's time to assess your resources – the fuel that keeps your content engine running. Do you have access to skilled writers, editors, and tech wizards? Can you adapt your service to meet specific needs? Is your resource chest overflowing with fresh ideas and the capacity to constantly update and improve? Remember, a well-oiled content machine is essential for staying ahead of the curve.

Customer Delight

Now, we shift gears to explore the engine that keeps your subscribers humming with satisfaction – exceptional customer service and fulfillment. Think of it as the secret sauce that transforms a good subscription site into a legendary one.

1. The Service Symphony: In the digital world, customer service is your stage, and every interaction a performance. Invest in building robust infrastructure that allows instant communication, swift problem -resolution, and proactive assistance. Remember, even the smallest hiccup can leave a lasting impression. So, orchestrate a symphony of seamless service, exceeding expectations with lightning-fast turnaround, competitive pricing, surprise extras, and generous guarantees.

2. From Satisfied Fans to Vocal Evangelists: When you consistently "wow" your customers, you ignite a powerful force – word-of-mouth referrals. These loyal fans become your unpaid marketing army, singing your praises and attracting new subscribers organically. They're the ultimate validation of your exceptional service, a testament to the joy you bring to their lives. Remember, happy customers aren't just metrics, they're the beating heart of your community.

3. Notifications and Automations: Implement a system to notify you or automatically respond to your customers. If you never miss a message, or set expectations of response with your customer, you build trust and loyalty.

Charting Your Course: Pricing Models and Revenue Streams for Your Thriving Site

The engine of your subscription site hums on a carefully crafted business model, and at its heart lies the crucial question: how do you make money? This section unpacks the treasure chest of revenue streams and pricing models, guiding you towards financial sustainability and growth.

Setting the Price - Unveiling Your Model: Determining your subscription rates and pricing model is like painting a roadmap to profitability. Research is your compass – delve into what your competitors charge and the services they offer. Remember, variety is key! Consider monthly, quarterly, and annual subscriptions, each with its own appeal. Experiment with one-time purchases for ebooks or downloadable content, allowing members to sample your expertise before diving deeper.

The Allure of Discounts: Loyalty deserves rewards! Offer enticing discounts for renewing members, like dropping the quarterly subscription from $19.95 to $16.95 for their next term. This fosters a sense of value and keeps them coming back for more.

Free vs. Premium - Striking the Balance: Should you lock everything behind a paywall, or entice with free samples? There's beauty in both! Free content acts as a magnet, drawing potential subscribers in, while premium offerings create exclusivity and deeper engagement. Strike a balance that showcases your value proposition without alienating free users. Many successful sites thrive on this hybrid model.

Beyond Subscriptions - Diversifying Your Income: Your revenue streams needn't be one-dimensional. Explore affiliate income, partnering with complementary products and services for commission opportunities. Offer exclusive coaching sessions or personalized consultations for dedicated members, adding a premium layer to your expertise. Think of your own ebooks, training materials, or online courses – your knowledge is a valuable asset! Workshops and boot camps for advanced subscribers can further diversify your income and deepen their learning.

Scaling Up - Building for Growth: One of the online world's magic tricks is the effortless scalability of your website. As your member base expands, ensure your software and databases can handle the surge. Keep your business model flexible, adapting to your members' needs as you scale.

Securing Funding - Fueling Your Journey: While bootstrapping is an option, venture capitalists and banks can be potential allies. Craft a compelling business proposal, highlighting your solid paid content model and well-executed plan. Remember, they need to see a clear path to profitability before they invest.

The Grand Finale: Exit in style. Many subscription sites experience dramatic success, leading to potential acquisitions by larger players in the market. Brick-and-mortar giants might even be interested in your digital haven! These lucrative exits pave the way for future ventures, fueled by the lessons learned and the success you've built.

By navigating these financial avenues with strategic planning and a clear vision, you'll not only build a thriving subscription site, but also lay the foundation for a sustainable and rewarding journey. Remember, your financial model is the grease of your digital kingdom – choose wisely, adapt creatively, and watch your online community flourish!

Charting Your Course:
A Navigator's Guide to Membership Website Platforms

The siren song of a thriving membership website beckons to many an entrepreneur and content creator. But like any voyage, setting sail requires a sturdy vessel and a reliable map. In this digital landscape, your vessel is your membership website platform, and your map is an understanding of the diverse options available. Fear not, intrepid explorer, for this guide will equip you with the knowledge to navigate both the WordPress and non-WordPress waters, helping you choose the platform that best suits your unique needs and ambitions.

WordPress:
The Familiar Seas of Open Source

For many, WordPress is a trusted port of call, its familiar interface and vast plugin ecosystem offering a sense of security and flexibility. Building a membership site with WordPress can be like cruising on a customizable galleon, allowing you to tailor the vessel to your specific cargo (content) and desired voyage (monetization strategies).

<u>Advantages</u> of <u>WordPress:</u>

Cost-effective: WordPress itself is free and open-source, making it a budget-friendly option for bootstrappers. Add to that the plethora of free plugins, and you can get your ship sailing without breaking the bank.

Scalability: From intimate fishing boats to bustling cruise liners, WordPress scales seamlessly. Whether you have a small, niche community or a global membership empire in mind, WordPress can handle the growth gracefully.

Customization: You're the captain! WordPress lets you personalize every aspect of your site, from the user interface to the functionality, with thousands of themes and plugins at your disposal.

Community and Support: No need to sail alone! The WordPress community is vast and incredibly helpful, offering forums, tutorials, and plugins tailored to membership websites.

Challenges of WordPress:

Technical learning curve: While user-friendly, WordPress doesn't steer itself. Expect some time upfront to familiarize yourself with the platform and potentially plugin configurations.

Security concerns: Open-source software comes with inherent security risks. Maintaining plugin updates and implementing security measures is crucial to keep your members' data safe.

Performance considerations: As your member base grows, performance can become an issue. Choosing optimized plugins and investing in proper hosting is essential for smooth sailing.

Non-WordPress: Exploring Uncharted Waters

Beyond the familiar shores of WordPress lie a vast ocean of dedicated membership website platforms, each offering unique features and functionalities. Consider them sleek, modern yachts, built specifically for smooth content delivery and monetization.

Popular Non-WordPress Platforms:

Kajabi: An all-in-one powerhouse, Kajabi combines website building, email marketing, course hosting, and community features in a user-friendly package. Ideal for creators offering courses, coaching programs, or exclusive content.

Thinkific: Another comprehensive platform, Thinkific emphasizes course creation and delivery, making it perfect for educators and thought leaders. Its drag-and-drop interface and robust marketing tools streamline the learning experience.

Podia: Simplicity is Podia's mantra. This platform focuses on clean design, easy course hosting, and seamless membership management, ideal for solopreneurs and creators with straightforward content offerings.

Mighty Networks: Community building takes center stage with Mighty Networks. This platform fosters engaged communities with forums, live chats, and group features, ideal for membership sites built around shared interests or hobbies.

Benefits of Non-WordPress Platforms:

Ease of use: Most non-WordPress platforms are designed for non-technical users, offering visual interfaces and drag-and-drop functionality. No coding required!

All-in-one solutions: Many platforms combine website building, marketing tools, community features, and payment gateways under one roof, simplifying your tech stack and workflow.

Scalability built-in: These platforms are designed to handle large member bases and high traffic, eliminating the need for complex plugin configurations or upgrades.

Security and reliability: With dedicated infrastructure and security measures, these platforms offer peace of mind, ensuring your members' data is safe and your site runs smoothly.

<u>Considerations for Non-WordPress Platforms:</u>

Locked-in ecosystems: Once on board, switching platforms can be challenging. Choose a platform with features that align with your long-term vision.

Subscription fees: These platforms usually have monthly or annual subscription fees, adding to your operational costs. Factor these in when budgeting for your site.

Limited customization: While offering flexibility, most platforms don't match the sheer customization potential of WordPress and its plugin ecosystem.

Choosing Your Compass:
Factors to Consider

With a map full of options, choosing the right platform can be daunting. But fear not, adventurer! Here are some key factors to consider to set your course:

Your budget: Determine your financial resources and compare platform costs, including subscription fees, transaction fees, and any necessary add-ons.

Your technical expertise: Assess your comfort level with technology. If you're a tech whiz, WordPress and its plugin world might be your playground. For less tech-savvy folks, the user-friendly interfaces of non-WordPress platforms like Podia or Kajabi might be more appealing.

Your content and offerings: What kind of content will you be offering? Courses, coaching programs, exclusive communities, or a combination? Choose a platform that caters to your specific content type and monetization strategies.

Scalability needs: Think about your future vision. Do you see your membership site growing into a bustling community of thousands? Opt for a platform that can handle future growth without requiring complex migrations or upgrades.

Community features: Will your site thrive on member interaction and engagement? Platforms like Mighty Networks excel in fostering vibrant communities with forums, live chats, and group features.

Integrations: Do you need your site to connect with other tools or services? Check for seamless integrations with email marketing platforms, payment gateways, or learning management systems.

Beyond the Platform:
Charting Your Course to Success

Choosing the right platform is just the first step on your membership site voyage. Remember, a sturdy vessel alone won't guarantee a smooth journey. To reach your destination of thriving community and financial success, here are some additional considerations:

Content is king: No matter how fancy your platform, it's the quality and value of your content that will captivate your members. Invest in creating engaging, informative, and valuable content that keeps them coming back for more.

Build your community: Foster interaction and engagement among your members. Encourage discussions, host live events, and create opportunities for connection. A vibrant community is the lifeblood of any successful membership site.

Market and promote: Don't wait for members to find you. Implement effective marketing strategies to reach your target audience and grow your membership base. Utilize social media, email marketing, and content marketing to spread the word about your offerings.

Analyze and adapt: Don't set course and forget it. Continuously monitor your site's performance, track member engagement, and adapt your strategies based on data. Be flexible and willing to evolve as your community and the online landscape change.

Setting Sail:
Bon Voyage!

With a well-chosen platform, valuable content, and a commitment to community building, your membership site is poised for success. So, chart your course, raise your sails, and embark on this exciting journey. Remember, the digital seas are full of opportunities, and with the right map and the wind in your sails, you'll reach your destination of a thriving community and rewarding business. Bon voyage, navigator!

Building Your Digital Citadel: Mapping the Structure of Your Thriving Membership Website

Congratulations, intrepid adventurer! You've chosen your platform, your sails are unfurled, and the siren song of a thriving membership website beckons. But before you set course, the next crucial step is crafting the map of your digital domain – the sitemap. This blueprint will guide your members through the treasure trove of content and value you offer, ensuring their journey is smooth, engaging, and ultimately rewarding.

Unveiling the Essential Pages

Your sitemap is a compass, pointing members towards the key destinations within your digital kingdom. These essential pages form the bedrock of your offering:

Home Page: Your grand entrance! This page sets the tone for your entire site, introducing your brand, your mission, and the value you provide. Make it visually captivating, concise, and informative, with enticing calls to action directing members to explore further.

About Page: Peel back the curtain! Offer a glimpse into the human side of your venture. Share your story, your expertise, and the passion that fuels your content. This personal touch fosters trust and connection with your members.

Membership Page: The heart of your site! Showcase your membership plans, detailing the different tiers, features, and benefits each offers. Be clear, concise, and use compelling visuals to highlight the value proposition and entice potential members to sign up.

Content Hub: This is where your expertise shines! Whether it's blog posts, video tutorials, downloadable resources, or exclusive courses, this is where you deliver the promised value. Organize your content logically, making it easy for members to navigate and find what they need.

Community Hub: Foster a sense of belonging! Create a designated space for members to connect, interact, and share their experiences. Forums, discussion boards, live chats, and even virtual events can all contribute to a vibrant community atmosphere.

Member Profiles: Let members express themselves! Allow them to customize their profiles, share their interests, and connect with like-minded individuals. This personalization enhances engagement and encourages deeper participation.

Account Management: Empower your members! Provide a dedicated space for them to manage their subscriptions, update their details, and access invoices or receipts. Transparency and control build trust and satisfaction.

Contact Page: Open the door to communication! Make it easy for members to reach out with questions, feedback, or suggestions. A readily available contact page shows you value their input and are committed to their needs.

Charting the Navigational Seas

Your navigation is the ship's wheel, guiding members through your content with ease. Keep it intuitive and user-friendly, ensuring quick access to key pages and avoiding navigational dead ends.

Main Navigation: This should be present on every page, offering access to the core sections like Home, About, Membership, Content Hub, and Community Hub. Use clear, concise labels and consider drop-down menus for subcategories within each section.

Secondary Navigation: Depending on your content organization, you might need additional menus within specific sections. For example, within the Content Hub, you could have separate menus for different content types like blog posts, videos, and resources.

Search Bar: Offer a search function for members to quickly find specific content they're looking for. This is especially helpful for large websites with extensive libraries.

Breadcrumbs: Show members their current location within the site hierarchy. This provides context and avoids navigational confusion.

Designing for Content and Community

Beyond the page structure, consider the visual and functional aspects of each page layout. Remember, you're designing a digital haven for your members, so prioritize clarity, engagement, and ease of use.

Content Hierarchy: Use visual cues like headings, subheadings, bullet points, and images to break down text and create scannable content. This makes it easier for members to digest information and find what they need.

Call to Action Buttons: Prompt members to take the next step with clear and compelling call to action buttons. Whether it's signing up for a membership, accessing exclusive content, or joining a discussion, make it easy for them to engage with your offerings.

White Space and Visual Design: Don't overload your pages! Use ample white space and a clean layout to avoid visual clutter and enhance readability. Incorporate visuals like images, videos, and infographics to break up text and add visual interest.

Mobile Responsiveness: In today's mobile-first world, ensure your site adapts seamlessly to different screen sizes and devices. Responsive design is crucial for optimal user experience and accessibility.

Remember, your sitemap is not a static document. As your content and community evolve, it's natural for your site structure and navigation to adapt. Regularly review your analytics, gather feedback from members, and be open to making adjustments to keep your digital haven welcoming and enriching for all.

Navigating the Murky Waters: Legal and Compliance Considerations for Your Membership Site

Your membership site shimmers like a hidden island paradise, beckoning adventurers with the promise of knowledge, connection, and exclusive treasures. But before you raise the Jolly Roger and welcome your eager crew aboard, there's an often-overlooked territory you must chart: the murky waters of legal and compliance considerations. Fear not, captain! This chapter equips you with the essential compass and tools to navigate these waters with confidence, ensuring your digital kingdom rests on a foundation of legal soundness and protects your loyal crew.

Charting the Course:
Understanding Your Legal Landscape

Before diving in, understand the legal terrain you navigate. Every country and region has its own set of laws and regulations that govern online businesses. Research, research, research! Identify the specific laws applicable to your location, and consider consulting a legal professional to ensure your site complies with all relevant regulations. Here are some key areas to explore:

Data Privacy and Security: This is your treasure chest, so guard it fiercely! Familiarize yourself with data privacy laws like GDPR (General Data Protection Regulation) and CCPA (California Consumer Privacy Act) to understand how you collect, store, and use member data.

Implement robust security measures to safeguard sensitive information and prevent unauthorized access.

Intellectual Property: Your content, branding, and resources are your crown jewels. Copyright, trademark, and intellectual property laws protect your unique offerings. Understand how to register your intellectual property and utilize proper licensing when incorporating third-party materials.

Terms of Service and Privacy Policy: These are your legal maps, outlining the rights and responsibilities of both you and your members. Craft clear and concise documents that address user behavior, dispute resolution, and limitations of liability. Make sure they are easily accessible and readily understood by your crew.

Accessibility Standards: Ensure your digital kingdom welcomes everyone, not just a select few. Familiarize yourself with web accessibility guidelines like WCAG (Web Content Accessibility Guidelines) to make your site usable for users with disabilities, fostering inclusivity and building a diverse community.

Hoisting the Flag:
Essential Legal Compliance Measures

Knowledge is power, so arm yourself with these essential compliance measures:

Data Breach Notification: Accidents happen, but be prepared! Understand your obligation to notify authorities and affected members in case of a data breach, minimizing potential damage and protecting your reputation.

Children's Online Privacy Protection Act (COPPA): If your site caters to children, comply with COPPA regulations regarding data collection and parental consent. Protecting young adventurers!

Spam and Unsubscribe Laws: Don't become the dreaded pirate of unwanted emails! Familiarize yourself with anti-spam laws like CAN-SPAM to ensure your communication with members is welcome and respectful. Clearly display unsubscribe options and honor them promptly.

E-commerce Transactions: If you offer paid memberships or sell products, understand e-commerce regulations relating to online transactions, refunds, and consumer protection. Transparency and fair business practices build trust and loyalty.

Beyond the Checklist: Embracing Proactive Compliance

Compliance isn't a one-time voyage; it's an ongoing quest. Embrace these proactive strategies to stay ahead of the legal curve:

Regular Reviews and Updates: Laws evolve, so stay vigilant! Regularly review your legal documents and website practices to ensure compliance with any new regulations or industry standards.

Security Audits and Vulnerability Assessments: Invest in professional security audits to identify and address potential vulnerabilities before they become critical breaches. Think of it as patching up your ship's hull before setting sail.

Privacy Impact Assessments: If you process large amounts of member data, consider conducting privacy impact assessments to identify potential risks and implement appropriate safeguards. This demonstrates your commitment to data privacy and builds trust with your crew.

Seek Expert Guidance: When in doubt, consult with legal professionals! They can navigate the complex legal landscape and provide specialized advice to ensure your membership site sails smoothly through any legal challenges.

Remember the Crew: Transparency and Communication

Your members are your loyal crew, so treat them with respect and transparency. Here are some key practices:

Clear and Accessible Legal Documents: Present your Terms of Service, Privacy Policy, and other legal documents in plain language, avoiding jargon and legalese. Make them easily accessible and encourage members to familiarize themselves with these guidelines.

Open Communication about Data Practices: Be transparent about how you collect, use, and protect member data. Explain your privacy policies in clear and concise terms, and promptly address any questions or concerns your crew may have.

Feedback and Improvement: Encourage feedback on your legal documents and website practices. Actively listen to your members' concerns and suggestions, and be willing to adapt and improve your policies to better serve their needs.

Anchoring in Safe Harbor:
A Thriving Membership Community

Building a thriving membership site goes beyond just content and community. It goes beyond just content and community. It requires navigating the complex waters of legal and compliance considerations, ensuring your digital kingdom rests on a foundation of sound legal practices and protects your loyal crew. By charting your course, hoisting the flag of essential measures, and embracing proactive compliance, you can transform your site into a safe harbor where knowledge, connection, and transformation flourish.

Remember, legal compliance isn't just a burden; it's a necessary compass that guides you towards building a trustworthy, inclusive, and sustainable haven for your members. So, captain, raise your sails with confidence, knowing your digital kingdom rests on a bedrock of legal soundness, ready to welcome adventurers from far and wide to embark on a journey of growth and discovery within your secure and thriving online community.

Words That Captivate: Crafting Compelling Copy for Your Thriving Membership Site

You've built your digital vessel, plotted your course, and amassed a treasure trove of valuable content. But to entice adventurers aboard and fill your kingdom with loyal subjects, you need the captivating power of copywriting. This is where words become your tools, crafting messages that resonate, convert, and forge deep connections with your potential members.

Remember copywriting is about sales. In most cases, that means saying less.

Crafting the Compass: Unveiling Your Value Proposition

Your copy is the map that guides your audience through your site, highlighting the riches within. But before you weave your words, remember: clarity is key. Define your value proposition – the core benefit that sets your membership site apart from the vast digital ocean. What unique treasure do you offer? Is it exclusive expertise, a vibrant community, transformative learning, or access to insider secrets? Distill this essence into a clear, concise message that resonates with your target audience.

Charting the Course:
Where to Learn the Craft

Honing your copywriting skills takes practice and inspiration. Here are a few trusty lighthouses to guide your learning:

Copyblogger: This legendary blog is a treasure chest of insights on website copywriting, email marketing, and content marketing. Dive into their archives and webinars for actionable tips and expert advice.

Content Marketing Institute: This industry leader offers in-depth resources on content creation, audience engagement, and storytelling. Their blog, ebooks, and online courses can equip you with the knowledge to craft compelling narratives for your site.

AWAI: The American Writers & Artists Institute provides comprehensive courses and training programs specifically designed for aspiring and professional copywriters. Whether you're starting from scratch or seeking advanced techniques, AWAI can steer you in the right direction.

<u>Four books to read:</u>

The Brain Audit: Why Customers Buy (and Why They Don't) by Sean D Souza

The Adweek Copywriting Handbook: The Ultimate Guide to Writing Powerful Advertising and Marketing Copy from One of America's Top Copywriters by Joe Sugarman

My Life in Advertising by Claude Hopkins

The Ultimate Sales Letter, 4th Edition: Attract New Customers. Boost your Sales. by Dan S Kennedy

Recruiting Your Crew:
Hiring Copywriting Help

Sometimes, even the most intrepid adventurers need a seasoned crew. If you're seeking professional expertise, consider these trusty harbors:

Upwork & Fiverr: These online marketplaces connect you with freelance copywriters from around the world. Browse portfolios, compare rates, and find the perfect writer to tackle specific projects or ongoing content creation.

Content Marketing Agencies: Many agencies offer copywriting services as part of their broader content marketing strategy. This can be a good option if you need a comprehensive approach to your site's content and messaging.

Social Media Groups: Platforms like Facebook and LinkedIn host vibrant communities of copywriters and content creators. Post your project requirements, and let the talent come to you!

Five Calls to Action that Convert

Now, let's set sail with some high-converting calls to action (CTAs) that inspire your audience to dive headfirst into your membership site:

"Unlock the Vault: Join our Membership and Secure Your Exclusive Advantages Today!" This CTA creates a sense of urgency and exclusivity, highlighting the unique benefits available only to members.

"Chart Your Course to Success: Start Your Free Trial and Experience the Value for Yourself." Offering a free trial lowers the barrier to entry and allows potential members to see the magic firsthand.

"Don't Just Dream, Achieve: Invest in Your Growth with Our Premium Membership and Transform Your Potential." This CTA appeals to personal aspirations and emphasizes the transformative power of your content.

"Join the Tribe: Find Your Community and Unleash Your Potential in Our Thriving Membership Ecosystem." This message highlights the sense of belonging and mutual support your site offers, fostering a connection beyond just content.

"Limited Time Offer: Claim Your Founding Member Status and Enjoy Exclusive Perks and Lifetime Access!" Scarcity and exclusivity can be powerful motivators. This CTA leverages a limited-time offer to encourage immediate action.

Remember, your copywriting is not just about words; it's about building bridges. Craft messages that resonate with your audience's aspirations, address their pain points, and showcase the transformative power of your membership site. So, hoist the sails, unleash the power of your words, and welcome your loyal subjects aboard your thriving digital kingdom!

Securing the Golden Gates: Choosing the Right Payment Gateway for Your Membership Website

Your members are drawn by the glittering treasure trove of your content, captivated by the promises of knowledge, community, and transformation. But before they embark on their membership journey, there lies the crucial checkpoint: the payment gateway. This digital tollbooth determines how effortlessly your riches can be exchanged for membership, and choosing the right one is just as important as crafting captivating copy or building a user-friendly interface. Your treasure lies within the membership fees, so ensuring secure and seamless payment is paramount.

Choose a reliable payment gateway – your digital cash register – that meets your needs and those of your crew. Here are some key factors to consider:

Security and Fraud Prevention: Choose a gateway with robust security measures like PCI compliance and fraud detection tools to protect your members' sensitive financial information. Remember, their trust is your most valuable currency.

Subscription Management: Seamless integration with recurring billing is crucial. Look for a gateway that handles automatic subscription renewals, payment retries, and cancellations efficiently.

Transaction Fees and Payment Options: Compare transaction fees and offered payment methods like credit cards, debit cards, and even international payment options to cater to your diverse crew.

Integrations and Ease of Use: Ensure smooth integration with your membership platform and website. A user-friendly gateway simplifies financial management and keeps the onboarding process smooth for both you and your members.

Navigating the Options:
A Sea of Gateways Awaits

The online landscape teems with diverse payment gateways, each with its own strengths and quirks. Let's explore some prominent options, venturing beyond the previously mentioned ones and uncovering new possibilities:

Stripe: A popular choice for its ease of use, global reach, and robust feature set. Stripe integrates seamlessly with most membership platforms and offers flexible subscription plans, recurring billing, and secure payment processing.

Braintree: Another familiar name, Braintree boasts fast setup, fraud prevention tools, and support for multiple payment methods. Its integrations with various platforms make it a versatile option for diverse membership models.

PayPal: This household name offers convenience and familiarity, especially for international audiences. While offering basic integrations with some platforms, its subscription management features might require workarounds.

ThriveCart: This powerhouse platform combines payment processing with powerful marketing and sales automation tools. Its built-in funnel builder and membership features cater specifically to online entrepreneurs and course creators.

Clickbank: A veteran in the digital product space, Clickbank excels with secure processing, affiliate marketing tools, and global payment acceptance. Its integration options might be less extensive compared to other gateways.

Recurly: True to its name, Recurly focuses on simplifying recurring billing for membership sites. Its robust API, extensive integrations, and advanced subscription management features make it a favorite for complex membership models.

Chargebee: Another subscription-centric platform, Chargebee offers flexible billing options, dunning management, and detailed analytics. Its integrations with popular platforms like WordPress and Kajabi cater to a wide range of membership site needs.

Beyond the Gateway: Charting Your Path with Platform Integrations

The ideal payment gateway seamlessly integrates with your chosen membership platform, creating a smooth and effortless checkout experience for your members. Consider these factors when choosing your gateway:

Compatibility: Ensure your chosen platform and gateway have a documented and well-maintained integration. Look for reviews and testimonials from users about the integration's functionality and reliability.

Feature Compatibility: Not all integrations offer the same level of functionality. Some allow basic subscription setup, while others enable automatic upgrades, dunning management, and advanced data analysis. Choose a gateway that seamlessly integrates with your desired features.

Transaction Fees and Recurring Billing: Compare transaction fees, monthly fees, and any additional charges associated with recurring billing. Factor these costs into your pricing model to ensure profitability.

Remember, your payment gateway is more than just a tollbooth. It's a vital part of your member experience, impacting trust, convenience, and overall satisfaction. Choose wisely, ensuring your gate is secure, user-friendly, and compatible with your platform, allowing your members to embark on their journey with ease and unlock the treasures you offer.

Beyond the Walls: Venturing into New Horizons

As your membership site evolves, you might seek additional payment options or expand into new markets. Consider these gateways for specialized needs:

GoCardless: This gateway specializes in direct bank debit payments, offering faster processing and lower fees for recurring payments in specific regions like Europe.

Adyen: For global businesses catering to diverse payment preferences, Adyen offers a vast array of payment methods, including local wallets and alternative payment solutions.

Choosing the right payment gateway is a crucial step in building a thriving membership site. Remember, your ultimate goal is to create a seamless, secure, and enjoyable experience for your members. Analyze your platform, evaluate your budget, and prioritize the features that matter most to your specific needs. With careful consideration and a sprinkle of adventurous spirit, you'll discover the perfect payment gateway to guide your members through the golden gates and into the treasure trove of your digital kingdom.

From Booty to Balance: Financial Management and Member Services for Your Membership Site

Ah, the thrill of the chase! You've lured adventurers to your membership site, promising treasure chests overflowing with knowledge, connection, and exclusive perks. But before you bask in the glory of a thriving community, there's a crucial quest you must conquer: financial management and accounting. Fear not, captain! This chapter equips you with the tools and savvy to navigate the choppy waters of fiscal responsibility, ensuring your digital kingdom rests on a foundation of financial soundness and sails smoothly towards profitability.

Beyond the Member Gates: Building Your Digital Back-Office Fortress

Your membership website hums with activity, a bustling hub of engaged members and valuable content. But behind the gleaming facade lies the engine room, the digital back-office, where the gears of administration grind away, ensuring your kingdom runs smoothly. This crucial chapter delves into crafting a robust back-office, an administrative interface that empowers you to manage your members, curate your content, and keep your digital domain thriving.

Choosing the right administrative interface and CMS is a crucial step in setting up your membership site. Reconsider your needs, prioritize your functionalities, and explore platforms that offer flexibility, security, and user-friendly tools. Remember, your back-office is not just a dashboard; it's the command center from which you orchestrate your digital kingdom's success. Choose wisely, and may your digital engine hum with efficiency, empowering you to nurture your community, curate rich content, and secure your membership.

Commanding the Controls: Your Administrative Interface

Imagine a cockpit overlooking your digital landscape. Your administrative interface is that vantage point, a dashboard filled with tools and data, empowering you to navigate every aspect of your membership site. Consider these essential functionalities:

Member Management: Your members are your precious cargo. The interface should allow you to easily add, edit, and delete user accounts, assign roles and permissions, and track member activity. Imagine filtering by subscription levels, analyzing engagement metrics, and even exporting member data for targeted marketing campaigns.

Content Control Center: Your content is your crown jewel. The CMS (Content Management System) within your back-office should be your creative workshop. Craft blog posts, upload videos, schedule webinars, and manage downloadable resources, all with a user-friendly interface and flexible formatting options. Think drag-and-drop functionality, intuitive scheduling tools, and even version control for seamless content revisions.

Financial Command Center: Money matters! Track your financial health with real-time insights into subscription revenue, transaction fees, and chargebacks. Generate reports, analyze sales trends, and even manage tax settings, ensuring your financial engine runs smoothly.

Analytics and Insights: Knowledge is power! Delve into member engagement data, track page views, analyze content performance, and identify user behavior patterns. Your back-office should equip you with the tools to understand your audience, refine your offerings, and optimize your content for maximum impact.

Communication Hub: Stay connected with your members! Broadcast announcements, send targeted email campaigns, and respond to individual inquiries, all from within your back-office. Imagine crafting personalized newsletters, scheduling automated welcome emails, and even managing live chat sessions, fostering a close connection with your community.

Customization is Key: Tailoring Your Back-Office to Perfection

No two membership sites are alike. Your back-office should reflect your unique needs and workflow. Look for platforms that offer customization options, allowing you to:

Configure Dashboards: Prioritize the metrics and tools you use most frequently. Create custom dashboards that display the information you need at a glance, boosting your administrative efficiency.

Extend Functionality: Many platforms offer extension libraries or API integrations, allowing you to add custom features, automate tasks, and connect your back-office to other tools you use.

Branding and Personalization: Make your back-office your own! Customize the interface to match your brand colors and preferences, creating a familiar and comfortable workspace.

User Management:
Building a Secure Vault for Your Members

Your members entrust you with their data and access, so security is paramount. Look for platforms that offer robust user management features, including:

Secure Logins: Two-factor authentication and strong password encryption are essential for safeguarding member information.

Role-Based Access Control: Differentiate member roles and permissions. Grant moderators specific access to manage forums, while restricting administrative functionalities to trusted personnel.

Privacy Compliance: Ensure your platform meets relevant data privacy regulations. Look for GDPR and CCPA compliance features to protect your members' data.

The Content Management System:
Your Creative Canvas

The CMS within your back-office is where your content takes shape. Choose a platform that empowers your creativity and simplifies content management:

User-Friendly Interface: Even the most tech-savvy adventurers appreciate simplicity. Choose a CMS with an intuitive interface and drag-and-drop functionality, allowing you to focus on crafting compelling content, not wrestling with complex technical hurdles.

Formatting Options: Unleash your creative vision! Rich text editing tools, media embed options, and customizable layouts should be at your fingertips. Style your content, insert captivating visuals, and create a visually appealing experience for your members.

Scheduling and Version Control: Plan your content calendar, schedule future publications, and maintain version control for easy rollbacks and revisions. Your CMS should be your partner in creative collaboration and organized workflow.

Setting Sail with Support:
Charting the Course for Member Services

Your membership site hums with life, a buzzing haven of engaged members and valuable content. But just like any adventurer traversing uncharted waters, your crew will need support – a friendly voice to answer questions, troubleshoot issues, and ensure their journey is smooth and rewarding. This chapter dives into crafting a robust support system, a crucial safety net that bolsters member satisfaction and keeps your digital ship sailing ahead.

<u>Understanding Support Needs</u>

Before raising the sails, map the landscape of your members' potential needs. Consider these common touchpoints:

Onboarding and Activation: Guide new members through the initial hurdles, helping them set up accounts, access content, and understand your site's features.

Technical Support: Troubleshooting login issues, resolving formatting problems, and assisting with platform navigation are all essential services.

Content-Related Inquiries: Help members find specific resources, understand complex concepts, and answer questions about your offerings.

Billing and Subscription Management: Address subscription-related concerns, guide members through upgrade options, and handle potential payment issues.

Community Management: Foster a positive and respectful environment, moderate discussions, and address any conflicts or concerns within your member community.

Navigating the Trade Winds: Tools for Financial Tracking and Reporting

Financial data is your compass, guiding you towards informed decisions and ensuring your kingdom's prosperity. Invest in reliable financial tracking and reporting tools:

Accounting Software: Consider cloud-based accounting software specifically designed for membership sites. These platforms automate essential tasks like income and expense tracking, generating invoices and financial reports, and managing sales tax.

Analytics and Reporting: Dive deeper into your data! Utilize built-in or integrated analytics tools to track key metrics like member acquisition costs, churn rates, and lifetime value. These insights reveal trends, identify areas for improvement, and enable data-driven decision making.

Spreadsheets and Budgeting: While sophisticated tools are valuable, basic budgeting and forecasting with spreadsheets can be your first mate. Track projected income and expenses, create spending plans, and monitor your financial health against set goals.

Charting the Course: Essential Financial Management Practices

Beyond tools, wise financial practices are your rudder.

Accurate Recordkeeping: Every coin, every doubloon, must be accounted for. Implement a rigorous system for recording all income and expenses, from membership fees to website maintenance costs. Consistency and precision are key to understanding your financial landscape.

Tax Calculations and Compliance: Navigating the tax seas can be tricky. Understand your local tax regulations and obligations, ensure you collect and remit sales tax as needed, and consider seeking professional tax advice to avoid unwanted surprises.

Cash Flow Management: Don't let your coffers run dry! Monitor your cash flow, prioritize expenditures, and plan for potential fluctuations in income. Consider buffer funds to weather unexpected financial storms and ensure your site's smooth operation.

Financial Forecasting and Projections: Look beyond the horizon! Utilize your financial data and industry trends to forecast future income and expenses. This allows you to set realistic budget goals, make informed investment decisions, and plan for sustainable growth.

Beyond the Numbers:
Human Connection and Trust

Financial management isn't just about numbers; it's about trust and transparency with your crew. Here are some additional tips:

Member Invoices and Statements: Provide clear and detailed invoices and account statements to your members. Transparency fosters trust and ensures your crew understands their financial commitments.

Open Communication and Reporting: Share key financial metrics with your members, even in challenging times. Open communication builds trust and demonstrates your commitment to financial responsibility.

Consider Professional Audits: As your membership site grows, consider engaging a financial professional for regular audits. This safeguards against inaccuracies, identifies potential risks, and provides valuable insights for optimizing your financial practices.

Anchoring in Prosperity:
A Financially Sustainable Kingdom

Remember, financial management isn't about hoarding treasure; it's about nurturing your digital kingdom's sustainable growth. By choosing the right payment gateway, leveraging financial tracking tools, and implementing sound financial practices, you can navigate the choppy waters of membership site finances with confidence. This ensures your digital haven remains a thriving community where knowledge, connection, and exclusive perks flourish alongside financial stability and trust. So, captain, chart your course with fiscal savvy, raise the sails of informed decision-making, and set course towards a prosperous future for your membership site and its loyal crew.

Building the Lighthouse: Setting Up Efficient Support Channels

Multiple channels cater to diverse needs:

Ticketing System: A robust ticketing system allows members to submit detailed inquiries and track their resolution progress. Offer email integration and self-service options for streamlined communication.

Live Chat: Real-time assistance for urgent questions or technical difficulties. Consider offering limited hours or blending AI chatbots with human support for optimal efficiency.

Knowledge Base: Compile FAQs, tutorials, and helpful guides. Empower members to find answers independently and reduce repeat inquiries.

Community Forum: Foster peer-to-peer support and encourage members to answer questions and share their knowledge, building a collaborative and supportive community spirit.

Raising the Jolly Roger: Embracing the Human Touch

Automation is vital, but remember, your members are not just data points. Inject a human touch into your support:

Personalized Responses: Go beyond canned scripts. Take the time to understand each member's needs and provide tailored solutions.

Empathy and Active Listening: Show genuine concern and actively listen to their concerns. Building rapport fosters trust and loyalty.

Timely Response: Aim for prompt resolutions. Set clear expectations and communicate response timelines, reassuring members their needs are heard.

Positive Language and Tone: Maintain a friendly and professional demeanor, even during challenging situations. Remember, your words can influence the entire member experience.

Beyond the Horizon: Proactive Support and Feedback

<u>Anticipate</u> <u>needs</u> <u>and</u> <u>actively</u> <u>engage</u> <u>members:</u>

Proactive Outreach: Reach out to new members, offering guidance and support during their initial journey. Conduct regular satisfaction surveys and gather feedback to identify areas for improvement.

Community Events and Webinars: Host live Q&A sessions, workshops, or social events to connect with your members on a deeper level, showcase your expertise, and encourage engagement.

Member Benefits and Rewards: Reward loyal members with exclusive perks, early access to content, or special discounts. Show appreciation for their commitment and foster a sense of belonging.

Building a Thriving Ecosystem of Support

Remember, your support system is not an isolated department. Integrate it seamlessly with your content and community efforts:

Content Integration: Weave support resources into your website. Embed FAQs within relevant sections, link to tutorials from specific courses, and offer clear contact options on every page.

Community Moderation: Empower your community leaders to answer questions and offer peer support. Train them on your policies and guidelines to ensure consistent quality and maintain a positive community environment.

Data-Driven Insights: Analyze support channels, track common inquiries, and identify recurring issues. Use this data to improve your content, refine your platform, and proactively address members' needs.

Crafting a robust support system is an investment in your members' satisfaction and ultimately, the success of your membership site. With a well-equipped back-office, efficient communication channels, and a human-centered approach, you can build a loyal community, navigate through any stormy seas, and ensure your digital ship sails to ever-brighter horizons. May your members' journey be smooth, rewarding, and forever guided by the supportive glow of your lighthouse.

A Maintenance Masterplan

Think of your website as a living, breathing entity. It requires regular upkeep to thrive, from polishing its visual sheen to safeguarding its technological underbelly. Consider these essential tasks in your maintenance plan:

Content Audits: Regularly review your content for accuracy, relevance, and engagement. Update information, refresh outdated formats, and cull irrelevant material to keep your offerings fresh and valuable.

Platform Updates: Stay ahead of the curve! Update your platform and plugins as soon as new versions become available. These updates often include security patches, performance improvements, and new features that can enhance your site's functionality.

Security Monitoring: Your members entrust you with their data. Implement robust security measures, including regular malware scans, strong passwords, and data backups. Stay vigilant against potential threats and prioritize data security in your maintenance plan.

Performance Optimization: Ensure your website sails smoothly! Monitor loading times, identify bottlenecks, and optimize images and code to ensure members enjoy a fast and seamless browsing experience.

Broken Link Patrol: Broken links are like navigational dead ends, frustrating members and damaging your site's credibility. Regularly check for broken links, fix them promptly, and consider implementing link redirection to minimize disruption.

SEO Savvy: Stay visible in the digital ocean! Employ search engine optimization (SEO) best practices, including keyword research, meta descriptions, and content optimization, to ensure your website ranks high in search results and attracts new adventurers to your shores.

Beyond the Checklist: Proactive Maintenance

A vigilant adventurer anticipates challenges before they arise. Proactive maintenance goes beyond ticking boxes, fostering a culture of constant improvement:

Analytics Insights: Don't just track data, glean insights! Analyze website traffic, engagement metrics, and member behavior patterns to identify areas for improvement, optimize content performance, and refine your overall strategy.

Testing and Experimentation: Never stop innovating! Experiment with new features, test different layouts, and gather member feedback to see what resonates and what needs adjustment. Be willing to adapt and evolve your website to remain relevant and engaging.

Security Audits: Schedule regular security audits conducted by professionals. These audits can identify vulnerabilities in your system and recommend proactive measures to keep your members' data safe.

Staying Educated: The digital landscape is ever-changing. Stay updated on industry trends, emerging technologies, and platform advancements. Continuous learning ensures your maintenance practices remain effective and your website stays ahead of the curve.

Remember the Crew: Teamwork for Website Wellness

Maintaining a website is not a solo voyage. Consider these strategies for a smoother journey:

Delegation and Outsourcing: Can't do it all alone? Delegate tasks to your team based on their strengths and expertise. Outsource specific elements like security audits or SEO optimization to qualified professionals, freeing up your time for other crucial aspects of your membership site.

Community Feedback: Your members are your most valuable resource. Encourage feedback, suggestions, and bug reports. Their insights can help you identify maintenance needs and prioritize improvements that directly benefit their experience.

Collaborative Tools: Utilize project management tools, communication platforms, and shared documents to keep your team on the same page. Collaborative practices ensure efficient maintenance workflows and streamline the upkeep of your digital kingdom.

Website management and maintenance are not just technical chores; they are the building blocks of a thriving membership site. By proactively tending to your website's health, you ensure a seamless user experience, safeguard your members' data, and keep your content fresh and engaging.

Remember, this is not a one-time voyage, but an ongoing quest for optimization and improvement. With a well-defined maintenance plan, a proactive approach, and a collaborative spirit, you can keep your website sailing smoothly, ensuring your members' journey within your digital kingdom is one of continual value, discovery, and delight. May your ship forever gleam with the polished touch of dedicated maintenance.

Hoisting the Jolly Roger: Sailing the Seas of Membership Site Promotion

Your membership site beckons adventurers from the vast digital ocean, promising transformation, connection, and the key to unlocking their potential. But like a hidden cove untouched by cartographers, your haven needs guidance – a robust plan for promotion, marketing, and advertising to draw eager explorers to its shores. This chapter equips you with the tools and savvy to navigate the turbulent waters of online marketing, attract loyal crewmates to your membership site, and watch your digital kingdom flourish.

Charting the Course: Understanding Your Audience

Before raising the sails, know your target audience. Imagine their aspirations, frustrations, and online habits. Are they seasoned professionals seeking career advancement? Aspiring artists yearning for creative inspiration? Busy parents juggling responsibilities and seeking self-care? Craft buyer personas – detailed profiles outlining their demographics, behaviors, and online pain points. This understanding guides your promotional efforts, ensuring your message resonates and your offerings provide solutions they desperately seek.

Unfurling the Banner:
Content Marketing for Organic Growth

Content is your compass, drawing adventurers towards your treasure trove. Craft compelling content that educates, inspires, and showcases the value your membership offers:

Blog Posts: Share your expertise, address your audience's challenges, and establish yourself as a thought leader. Weave in subtle promotional calls to action, inviting readers to delve deeper into your membership content.

Podcasts and Webinars: Engage your audience with interactive formats. Offer actionable tips, host Q&A sessions, and interview guest experts to showcase your knowledge and the diversity of your offerings.

Social Media: Foster interaction on platforms your audience frequents. Share insightful posts, engage in conversations, and run interactive contests or challenges to build a community around your brand.

Infographics and Videos: Break down complex concepts into visually engaging formats. Infographics offer bite-sized information, while videos can demonstrate your unique teaching style and connect with your audience on a personal level.

Spreading the Word:
Paid Advertising for Targeted Reach

Organic reach has its limitations. Paid advertising lets you target specific demographics and interests, placing your promotional message directly before your ideal audience. Consider these platforms:

Search Engine Marketing (SEM): Bid on relevant keywords to ensure your website appears at the top of search results when potential members seek solutions you offer.

Social Media Advertising: Tailor your ads to specific demographics and interests, ensuring your message reaches the right people on platforms like Facebook, Instagram, and LinkedIn.

Display Advertising: Target websites your audience frequents with banner ads or sponsored content, subtly reminding them of your offerings across the digital landscape.

Beyond the Horizon:
Beyond the Usual Suspects

Don't limit yourself to conventional channels. Explore these unconventional, yet impactful, avenues:

Collaborations and Partnerships: Partner with complementary businesses or influencers to reach new audiences. Co-host webinars, create joint content, or offer cross-promotional deals to expand your reach and leverage established communities.

Affiliate Marketing Program: Enlist passionate individuals to promote your membership site in exchange for a commission. Provide them with unique tracking links and marketing materials to incentivize their efforts and broaden your reach.

Guest Blogging and Podcasts: Offer your expertise to relevant blogs and podcasts. Share valuable insights, subtly highlighting your membership site as the ultimate resource for deeper knowledge and transformation.

Treasured Tips and Tricks: Sailing Smoothly Through the Marketing Seas

Here are some handy tools and strategies to navigate the digital waters:

Landing Page Optimization: Craft dedicated landing pages for each promotional campaign, focusing on a single benefit and offering a clear call to action. A/B test different headlines, call-to-action buttons, and layouts to refine your landing pages for maximum conversion.

Email Marketing: Nurture leads with targeted email sequences. Offer valuable freebies, share exclusive content, and gently guide potential members towards joining your membership site. Segment your email list to personalize your messaging and address specific needs.

Lead Magnets and Free Trials: Offer valuable resources like ebooks, checklists, or short video tutorials in exchange for email addresses. These opt-in incentives allow you to build your email list and nurture potential members who may not be ready to commit to a full membership initially. Free trials, with clear end dates and easy opt-out options, provide a low-risk way for potential members to experience the value your site offers, leading to higher conversion rates.

Contests and Giveaways: Generate excitement and attract new followers with engaging contests and giveaways. Offer exclusive membership access as prizes, incentivizing participation and spreading awareness.

Testimonials and Case Studies: Leverage the power of social proof! Share genuine testimonials from satisfied members, showcasing the real-world results and transformations your membership site offers. Case studies highlighting specific success stories add credibility.

Following the Trade Winds:
Tracking and Analyzing Your Marketing Voyage

Your promotional sails are filled, propelling your membership site towards a flourishing future. But like any seasoned captain, you need to navigate with precision. Tracking and analyzing your marketing efforts equips you with vital data, revealing what works, what needs adjustment, and ensuring your precious marketing resources are invested wisely.

Unfurling the Maps:
Essential Metrics to Track

Metrics are your compass, guiding you through the data-driven landscape. Track these key indicators to gauge the effectiveness of your promotional campaigns:

Website Traffic: Monitor overall website traffic and identify which channels drive the most visitors. Understand which content resonates with your audience and attracts new adventurers.

User Engagement: Analyze time spent on site, page views per session, and bounce rate to gauge how engaged your audience is with your content. Identify sections that require improvement or call to action that need refinement.

Lead Generation: Track opt-in rates for email lists, webinar registrations, and downloaded freebies. Measure the effectiveness of your lead magnets and capture forms to optimize your lead generation funnel.

Conversion Rates: Track the percentage of visitors who convert into paying members. Analyze which promotional channels and landing pages deliver the highest conversion rates, allowing you to double down on what works best.

Customer Lifetime Value (CLV): Understand the average revenue generated by each member over their lifetime. CLV helps you prioritize retention strategies and measure the long-term profitability of your membership site.

Tools of the Trade: Navigating the Data Seas

Embrace these analytics tools to decipher the messages within your data:

Website Analytics Platforms: Google Analytics is a powerful tool for tracking website traffic, user behavior, and conversions. Utilize its data to understand visitor journey and optimize your website for increased engagement.

Social Media Insights: Most social media platforms offer built-in analytics tools. Track post reach, engagement metrics, and follower demographics to tailor your social media strategy to resonate with your target audience.

Email Marketing Platforms: These platforms provide detailed analytics on email open rates, click-through rates, and unsubscribe rates. Utilize this data to refine your email campaigns, segment your list effectively, and increase email engagement.

Conversion Tracking Tools: Tools like ClickFunnels and Leadpages help you track conversions across different landing pages and marketing channels. These insights identify the most effective paths to membership and allow you to optimize your promotional efforts for maximum conversions.

Beyond the Numbers:
Qualitative Insights for Deeper Understanding

Data tells a story, but sometimes you need to hear it from the source. Qualitative insights add depth and nuance to your understanding of your audience:

Customer Surveys and Feedback: Ask your members and website visitors for their honest feedback. Learn about their pain points, expectations, and what motivates them to engage with your content or join your membership site.

Social Media Interactions: Monitor comments and conversations on your social media channels. Identify common themes, concerns, and areas of interest, allowing you to tailor your outreach and content to directly address their needs.

Focus Groups and Interviews: Gather a small group of target audience members for in-depth discussions. Understand their motivations, challenges, and perceptions of your brand and offerings. This can provide valuable insights into how to refine your messaging and cater to their specific needs.

A Voyage of Continuous Improvement:
Optimizing Your Course

Data and insights are not trophies; they are tools for continual improvement. Implement these strategies to refine your marketing strategy based on your findings:

A/B Testing: Test different headlines, call-to-action buttons, landing page layouts, and email subject lines to see what resonates best with your audience. Adapt your marketing materials based on data-driven insights to optimize performance.

Personalization: Leverage your data to personalize your outreach. Segment your audience based on demographics, interests, and engagement levels, and tailor your marketing messages and offerings to their specific needs.

Content Refinement: Analyze user engagement with your content. Identify popular topics and formats, and refine your content strategy to focus on the content that resonates most with your audience.

Channel Revamp: Based on your data, prioritize the marketing channels that deliver the highest return on investment. Invest more resources in channels that generate significant traffic, leads, and conversions, while adjusting or even abandoning channels that underperform.

Anchoring in Success:
A Thriving Membership Community

Effective promotion, marketing, and advertising are not just about attracting new members. They are about building a thriving community around your membership site. By leveraging data, insights, and continuous optimization, you can ensure your promotional efforts reach the right audience, resonate with their needs, and ultimately guide them towards the transformational treasures within your digital kingdom. With savvy marketing at your helm, your membership site will sail towards ever-brighter horizons, forever attracting eager crewmates.

From Scallywags to Shipmates: Team Management and Collaboration for Your Membership Site

Ah, the thrill of the pirate life is infectious! You've assembled a motley crew of talented adventurers, each with their unique skills and expertise, drawn to the treasures within your vibrant membership site. Yet, managing this eclectic band of swashbucklers requires more than just a hearty "Yarrr!" This chapter equips you with the necessary tools and strategies to navigate the sometimes-choppy waters of team management and collaboration, transforming your crew into a well-oiled machine and ensuring your digital kingdom sails towards smooth and successful operation.

Hoisting the Colors: Defining Roles and Workflows

A crew without defined roles is like a ship without a map – destined for chaos. Clearly assign responsibilities to each team member based on their strengths and expertise. Consider roles like:

Content Captain: Curates and creates high-quality content, from articles and videos to webinars and interactive modules.

Community Navigator: Fosters member engagement through forums, live events, and personalized interactions.

Technical Officer: Maintains the website and membership platform, ensuring smooth operation and troubleshooting technical hiccups.

Marketing Buccaneer: Spreads the word about your site through targeted campaigns and promotional strategies.

Financial Helmsman: Tracks income and expenses, manages budgets, and oversees financial aspects of the site.

Once roles are set, establish defined workflows for each task. Outline clear steps for content creation, member onboarding, technical problem -solving, and other essential processes. Streamlining workflows ensures consistent quality, avoids confusion, and keeps your crew working efficiently.

Charting the Course: Collaborative Communication and Feedback

Clear communication is the lifeblood of any successful team. Establish open and accessible communication channels like email, online chat platforms, or project management tools. Encourage regular communication, updates, and information sharing to keep everyone on the same page.

Embrace the power of feedback. Create a culture where constructive criticism is welcomed and acted upon. Regular feedback sessions, peer reviews, and performance evaluations help individuals grow, identify areas for improvement, and strengthen the overall team dynamic. Remember, even the smoothest sailing requires adjustments to the sails based on feedback and changing winds.

Navigating the Storms:
Conflict Resolution and Team Wellness

Even the most harmonious crews can encounter squalls. Be prepared to handle conflict resolution situations with a calm and objective approach. Establish clear guidelines for addressing disagreements, encourage respectful communication, and focus on finding solutions that benefit the team and the site.

Prioritize team wellness as well. Encourage work-life balance, celebrate successes, and acknowledge individual and team contributions. Create opportunities for team bonding and informal interactions to build camaraderie and foster a positive and supportive environment. Remember, happy and well-rested pirates are the most productive pirates!

Beyond the Crew:
Tools and Technologies for Collaborative Power

In today's digital age, a plethora of tools can enhance your team's ability to collaborate:

Project Management Platforms: Keep track of tasks, deadlines, and progress with tools like Asana, Trello, or Monday.com. These platforms facilitate communication, assign responsibilities, and ensure everyone is working towards the same goals.

Cloud-Based Document Sharing: Collaborate on documents effortlessly with platforms like Google Docs or Dropbox. These tools allow real-time editing, version control, and accessibility from anywhere, making revisions and team collaboration seamless.

Communication and Video Conferencing Tools: Stay connected and hold productive meetings even remotely with tools like Zoom, Slack, or Google Meet. These platforms enable video conferencing, instant messaging, and file sharing, keeping your crew in sync and engaged.

Anchoring in Success: A United and Effective Team

Building a thriving membership site isn't a solo voyage; it's a collaborative adventure. By clearly defining roles, establishing efficient workflows, embracing open communication and feedback, and leveraging technology to your advantage, you can transform your crew of individual adventurers into a united and effective team. Remember, a well-managed team is like a well-oiled ship – ready to weather any storm, navigate uncharted waters, and secure a treasure trove of success for your digital kingdom and its loyal members. So, raise the Jolly Roger of collaboration, captain, and set sail towards a future where your site flourishes under the guidance of a skilled and united crew!

Beyond the Open Seas: Advanced Strategies for Membership Site Sustainability

You've navigated the choppy waters of promotion, crafted a content-rich treasure trove, and built a loyal crew of adventurers eager to unlock your knowledge and support. But just like any captain charting uncharted waters, you need to look beyond the immediate horizon. This chapter delves into advanced strategies for membership site sustainability, ensuring your digital kingdom thrives over time, weathering market storms, and continuously adapting to the evolving needs of your community.

Charting the Long Course: Building Recurring Revenue and Retention

Membership sites rely on sustained engagement and active subscriptions. Implement these strategies to cultivate a loyal community and secure recurring revenue:

Recurring Billing Optimization: Offer flexible subscription plans and pricing options to cater to diverse budgets and commitment levels. Consider annual memberships, tiered access levels, or bundled packages to incentivize long-term commitment.

Member Value and Engagement: Continuously deliver premium content, exclusive resources, and unparalleled member experiences that justify the ongoing subscription fee. Host live workshops, Q&A

sessions, and member-only events to foster deeper engagement and community connections.

Personalized Communication and Support: Treat your members as valued individuals. Offer personalized onboarding experiences, tailored recommendations, and prompt support to address their needs and ensure satisfaction. Remember, happy members are loyal members.

Community Building and Incentives: Foster a collaborative and supportive environment. Encourage peer-to-peer learning, host member forums, and celebrate member achievements. Consider gamification elements and loyalty programs to incentivize ongoing engagement and community participation.

Navigating the Currents:
Adapting to Change and Embracing Innovation

The digital landscape is dynamic. Membership sites that stay stagnant risk being swept away by the tide. Embrace these strategies to adapt and thrive:

Content Refresh and Expansion: Don't let your content become stale. Regularly update existing resources, introduce new formats, and experiment with innovative content types like interactive modules, live streams, or virtual reality experiences.

Market Trends and Member Feedback: Stay attuned to industry trends and evolving member needs. Conduct surveys, host focus groups, and actively seek feedback to understand what resonates and identify areas for improvement.

Technology Embracement: New technologies can enhance your offerings and streamline operations. Explore tools for automated email sequences, personalized recommendations, or AI-powered chatbots to provide efficient and engaging member experiences.

Collaborations and Partnerships: Partner with complementary businesses or influencers to expand your reach, cross-promote offerings, and access new market segments. Strategic collaborations can open new doors and breathe fresh life into your membership site.

Weathering the Storms:
Crisis Management and Risk Mitigation

Even the smoothest voyages can encounter unexpected challenges. Be prepared to navigate potential pitfalls with these strategies:

Data Security and Privacy: Implement robust security measures to safeguard member data. Regularly update software, conduct security audits, and prioritize data privacy to build trust and prevent reputation damage.

Technical Challenges and Outages: Technology can malfunction. Have a contingency plan for website outages, data breaches, or technical glitches. Communicate transparently with your members, prioritize swift resolution, and minimize disruption to maintain their trust and loyalty.

Reputation Management: Negative feedback can happen. Actively monitor online reviews and address concerns promptly. Be open to constructive criticism and use it as an opportunity to improve your offerings and member experience.

Community Moderation and Conflict Resolution: Foster a respectful and inclusive online environment. Establish clear community guidelines, address conflicts impartially, and empower members to report inappropriate behavior to maintain a positive and welcoming atmosphere.

Anchoring in Success:
A Legacy of Transformation and Connection

Building a sustainable membership site goes beyond revenue generation. It's about creating a legacy of transformation, connection, and lasting value for your members. By focusing on recurring revenue, adapting to change, and weathering potential storms, you can ensure your digital kingdom stands strong against the tides of time. Remember, your members are your compass, your community your sails, and your ongoing quest for innovation the wind that propels you forward. So, captain, set your course with confidence, steer towards a flourishing future, and leave an indelible mark on the digital seas with a membership site that empowers, transforms, and forever resonates with your loyal crew.

Beyond the Horizon: Scaling and Growth Strategies for Your Membership Site

Your membership site shimmers like a hidden archipelago, a haven of knowledge, connection, and exclusive treasures, drawing an ever-growing wave of adventurers to its shores. But like any ambitious captain, you know true success lies not just in building your island paradise, but in boldly venturing beyond the horizon, navigating the currents of scaling and growth. This chapter equips you with the essential compass and tools to chart your course towards a thriving digital kingdom, forever expanding its reach and enriching the lives of its loyal crew.

Hoisting the Sails: Defining Your Expansion Plans and Goals

Before setting sail, chart your course! Clearly define your expansion plans and goals. Do you aim to double your member base within a year? Target specific niche audiences? Introduce new premium membership tiers? Be specific, measurable, achievable, relevant, and time-bound (SMART) in your goals, ensuring your crew understands the direction and purpose of your voyage.

New Lands to Explore: Identifying Growth Opportunities

Growth lies not just in numbers, but in expanding your offerings and diversifying your horizons. Consider these strategies:

Content Diversification: Go beyond your comfort zone! Supplement your existing content with engaging formats like podcasts, interactive modules, live workshops, or even virtual reality experiences. Cater to diverse learning styles and keep your members perpetually on the edge of discovery.

Strategic Partnerships: Forge alliances with complementary businesses or influencers. Cross-promote offerings, reach new audiences, and leverage your combined expertise to expand your community and enhance member value.

Community Expansion: Foster a vibrant and interconnected community. Facilitate member-to-member interactions through forums, online events, and mentorship programs. Remember, your members are your greatest marketing asset – empower them to become ambassadors of your site.

Monetization Strategies: Explore new revenue streams beyond basic subscriptions. Offer exclusive product discounts, merchandise, paid guest speakers, or premium content packages. Tailor your offerings to cater to different member needs and willingness to invest.

Charting the Course: Building Scalable Systems and Processes

Growth can be exhilarating, but also overwhelming. Prepare your ship for choppy waters by establishing scalable systems and processes:

Automation wherever possible: Invest in tools to automate routine tasks like email marketing, member onboarding, and basic customer service inquiries. This frees up your time and resources for strategic initiatives and fostering deeper connections with your members.

Streamlined Workflows: Optimize your internal processes for efficiency. Refine content creation pipelines, delegate tasks effectively, and utilize project management tools to keep your team organized and on track.

Technology Investments: Don't let outdated infrastructure anchor you down. Invest in scalable hosting solutions, robust website security measures, and data management tools to handle increased traffic and member data securely.

Weathering the Storms: Challenges and Risks of Growth

Growth brings not just rewards, but potential pitfalls. Be prepared to navigate these challenges:

Managing Churn: As your site expands, keeping your existing members engaged can become more challenging. Develop retention strategies like personalized recommendations, exclusive loyalty programs, and ongoing value creation to solidify member commitment.

Maintaining Community Quality: Ensure your thriving community doesn't become a chaotic sea. Implement clear guidelines for member behavior, address conflicts promptly, and actively cultivate a welcoming and inclusive environment.

Staying Agile and Adaptable: The digital landscape is dynamic. Be prepared to adapt your strategies to changing trends, new technologies, and member feedback. Don't be afraid to course-correct, experiment with new ideas, and stay ahead of the curve.

Anchoring in Success:
A Legacy of Growth and Impact

Scaling your membership site isn't just about numbers; it's about creating a legacy of growth and impact. Remember, your true treasure lies in the transformative experiences you offer, the connections you forge, and the lives you enrich through your ever-expanding digital kingdom. By setting clear goals, exploring new horizons, building scalable systems, and navigating potential challenges, you can ensure your site sails towards a future of sustainable growth, leaving a lasting mark on the lives of your loyal crew and the wider online community.

So, captain, raise the Jolly Roger of ambition, unfurl the sails of innovation, and embark on a voyage of boundless expansion. Chart your course with confidence, knowing that your commitment to growth, along with the unwavering support of your crew, will guide your membership site towards uncharted waters of success, enriching the lives of your members and leaving an indelible mark on the digital sea.

Sunset on the Horizon: Exit Strategies for Your Membership Site

Your membership site, once a fledgling island paradise, has blossomed into a thriving archipelago, teeming with knowledge, connection, and loyal crewmates. Yet, even the most epic sagas must eventually reach their final chapter. This chapter delves into the often overlooked, but crucial realm of exit strategies, equipping you, captain, with the tools and foresight to navigate your digital kingdom's future, ensuring a smooth transition and lasting legacy, regardless of whether you seek new horizons or pass the helm to a worthy successor.

Hoisting the Compass: Charting Potential Courses

Every journey has its end, and every captain must consider the destination. Begin by charting potential courses for your site's future:

Selling the Kingdom: If new adventures beckon, consider selling your membership site. Conduct thorough valuations, research potential buyers, and ensure a smooth transition that prioritizes member well-being and data security. Remember, your loyal crew deserves a captain who steers them towards continued success.

Transferring the Crown Jewels: Perhaps legacy beckons. Transferring ownership to a trusted successor can ensure your site's continuity. Develop a transparent succession plan, mentor your chosen heir, and prioritize a seamless transition that minimizes disruption for your crew.

Lowering the Jolly Roger: Should unforeseen circumstances prevail, you may need to close your site. Prioritize member communication, handle financial obligations ethically, and safeguard member data responsibly. Remember, even in closure, transparency and respect for your crew remain paramount.

Navigating the Currents: Handling Member Data and Obligations

No matter your chosen course, member data and financial obligations demand careful consideration:

Data Privacy and Security: Whether transferring ownership or closing your site, prioritize your crew's trust and adhere to data privacy regulations. Clearly communicate your plans, provide member data export options, and ensure its responsible deletion or transfer to the new captain.

Subscriptions and Refunds: Handle outstanding subscriptions ethically. Offer prorated refunds, grace periods, or migration options to similar platforms. Remember, leaving your crew stranded in financial uncertainty tarnishes your legacy.

Financial Responsibilities: Fulfill all financial obligations before setting sail for new shores. Settle outstanding debts, manage taxes ethically, and ensure your creditors are informed and satisfied. Remember, leaving a clean financial wake preserves your reputation and protects your crew's interests.

Plotting the Future:
Succession Planning for a Legacy

If passing the captain's hat to a successor is your chosen course, succession planning becomes your guiding star:

Identify the Next Captain: Choose a successor who embodies your values, possesses the necessary skills, and enjoys the trust of your crew. Look for leadership qualities, digital savvy, and genuine passion for your site's mission.

Knowledge Transfer and Mentoring: Share your knowledge and expertise generously. Develop training materials, create mentoring programs, and ensure your successor understands the inner workings of your digital kingdom. Remember, a smooth transition requires open communication and ongoing support.

Community Engagement and Transparency: Inform your crew about your succession plan. Introduce your chosen successor, highlight their qualifications, and facilitate the building of trust and confidence between them and the community. Remember, your crew deserves a say in the captain who steers them into the future.

Anchoring in Calm Waters:
A Smooth and Secure Ending

Regardless of your chosen course, the key to a successful exit lies in prioritizing a smooth and secure ending:

Communication and Transparency: Keep your crew informed throughout the process. Explain your reasons, outline the plan, and address their concerns openly and honestly. Remember, respect and clear communication are lifeboats that weather any storm.

Data Security and Member Well-being: Safeguard member data and prioritize their well-being above all else. Offer support, migration options, and transparent communication to minimize disruption and ensure their continued digital journeys.

Ethical and Responsible Practices: Conduct your exit with integrity. Fulfill financial obligations, treat your crew with respect, and leave your digital kingdom in a state of order and stability. Remember, your final act will forever be etched in the memories of your loyal crew.

Setting Sail for New Horizons

Sailing the seas of online communities is an epic adventure, one filled with moments of growth, joy, and connection. But every successful voyage must eventually reach its conclusion. By navigating the choppy waters of exit strategies with foresight, planning, and a commitment to the well-being of your crew, you can ensure a smooth transition, preserve your legacy, and set sail for new horizons, whether as a proud captain emeritus or a trusted mentor guiding the next generation towards their own digital kingdoms.

So, chart your course, captain, with your compass of planning and your sails of transparency, and remember, even in the final chapters of your site's story, respect, responsibility, and the spirit of adventure will will forever guide you and your loyal crew towards a rewarding end, leaving behind a legacy of knowledge, connection, and a vibrant digital haven that enriched countless lives.

Remember, captain, your impact transcends the sunset of your membership site, echoing in the memories and transformations of your crew, forever sailing the digital seas you helped them navigate. As you raise your final toast to your loyal adventurers, savor the journey, celebrate the successes, and embrace the new horizons that await you on the ever-unfurling map of your life.

Resources

Also available online: 42black.com/resources

Crave a Membership Site Masterclass?

Tucked away in the "Resources" section at the link above lies buried treasure: unlock more guiding secrets to building your own membership site.

Build It With WP (Video Course):

Master WordPress tech stack: plugins and platforms to leave tech woes behind and get started right now.

Membership Site Masterclass (Audio):

Dive deeper into the nitty-gritty of keeping members.

Free Downloads

You can download the following sections for free at the link above, but they are also available on the following pages. We may have added additional resources not listed here, too.

- ✧ 20 Questions to Choosing the Right Membership Model
- ✧ Choosing Your Tech Fleet
- ✧ Long-term Checklist
- ✧ Pirate of Progress Reminders

20 Questions to Choosing the Right Membership Model

Remember, there's no one-size-fits-all membership model. By taking the time to answer these questions and reflect on your goals, you can chart a course towards a thriving online membership that delivers value to your members and brings you closer to your own "Freedom Empire."

Target Audience:

1. Who are you trying to help?

2. What specific problem or desire do you solve for them?

3. What are their demographics and interests? (Age, location, income, online habits, pain points, etc.)

4. What level of expertise do they have in your niche? (Beginner, intermediate, advanced)

Content and Value:

5. What unique value can you offer through your membership?

6. What sets you apart from competitors?

7. What types of content will you create? (Articles, videos, podcasts, live events, workshops, etc.)

8. How often will you publish new content? (Daily, weekly, monthly)

9. Will you offer different tiers of membership with varying levels of access? (Exclusive content, one-on-one coaching, bonus materials, etc.)

Community and Engagement:

10. How will you foster a sense of community among your members? (Forums, live chats, Q&A sessions, member spotlights, etc.)

11. What opportunities will you offer for interaction and collaborations? (Masterminds, group projects, peer support groups, etc.)

12. How will you handle conflicts and disputes within the community? (Clear guidelines, moderation, dispute resolution process, etc.)

Business and Sustainability:

13. What will your pricing model be? (Monthly, annual, tiered memberships, one-time fees)

14. What payment methods will you accept? (Credit cards, PayPal, Stripe, other options)

15. What are your estimated costs for hosting, technology, and marketing?

16. How will you track your expenses and revenue? (Financial tracking tools, budgeting strategies, etc.)

Growth and Future-proofing:

17. What are your long-term goals for your membership site? (Building a community, generating income, creating a brand, etc.)

18. How will you scale your site to accommodate future growth? (Upgraded systems, automation tools, hiring a team, etc.)

19. How will you stay up-to-date with industry trends and member needs? (Research, competitor analysis, feedback surveys, etc.)

20. What is your backup plan if you need to take a break or leave the project? (Succession plan, automated systems, handover process, etc.)

Personal Motivation and Commitment:

21. Are you passionate about your niche and excited to create content for your members?

22. Are you committed to the long-term success of your site, even when faced with challenges?

Choosing Your Tech Stack

Remember, there's no one-size-fits-all answer. Carefully consider your needs, resources, and long-term goals to choose the tech setup that will help you navigate the digital seas smoothly and reach your desired destination.

Membership Site Platforms to Sail Your Digital Seas

All-in-One Solutions:

Kajabi: Powerful platform with all-in-one features (courses, landing pages, email marketing) but pricier. Best for established creators with diverse offerings.

Teachable: Popular choice for online courses with good community features and marketing tools. Great for course-centric memberships.

Podia: Simple and user-friendly interface, ideal for beginners and solo creators. Focuses on content delivery & sales, not advanced features.

Thinkific: Feature-rich platform for courses and memberships, offers advanced customization and integrations. Best for tech-savvy creators.

Memberful: Plugin for existing websites (WordPress, etc.) to add membership functionality. Cost-effective for simple memberships, limited scalability.

Simplero: Ideal for digital content and information sellers who don't want to juggle multiple tools to operate your membership site.

LearnWorlds: Powerful course creation tools, advanced marketing features, customizable design options, strong analytics.

Community-Focused Platforms:

Circle: Emphasis on fostering vibrant communities with forums, live chat, and social features. Strong for interactive, engagement-driven memberships.

Tribe: Members can use a white-labeled Tribe to ask questions, start discussions, share content, participate in polls, and more.

Mighty Networks: Combines courses, communities, and live events to create immersive learning experiences. Best for building exclusive, tight-knit groups.

BuddyBoss: WordPress plugin focused on building online communities with forums, groups, and social features. Good for existing WordPress users aiming for strong community.

WPForo: WordPress plugin for forums that is well integrated with Profile Builder and Paid Membership plugins, such as BuddyPress, Ultimate Members, WooCommerce Membership, MemberPress, and SureMembers plugins.

E-commerce & Content Subscription Platforms:

Substack: Text-based platform for writers and newsletter creators to offer paid subscriptions. Ideal for creators focused on written content.

Patreon: Membership platform for artists, creators, and musicians to receive recurring support from fans. Best for building a dedicated fan base.

Gumroad: Sell digital products and memberships with a focus on simplicity and direct sales. Easy to use but limited community features.

Budget-Friendly Options:

Wix: All-in-one website builder with basic membership functionality included in premium plans. Affordable but limited customization and scalability.

Weebly: Similar to Wix, offers basic membership features within website builder plans. Good for simple memberships on a budget.

Self-Hosted Solutions:

WordPress: Highly customizable and flexible, requires web hosting and plugin setup. Best for tech-savvy users with control over every aspect. (WordPress.org is not the final solution. Plugins are required to turn it into a membership site.)

WordPress Plugins

A. **Wishlist Member:** Focuses on powerful marketing tools for driving sales and conversions, including autoresponders, coupons, and memberships funnels.

B. **MemberPress:** Adds powerful membership features and content restriction.

C. **Paid Memberships Pro:** Simple and user-friendly interface, makes setting up your membership site straightforward.

D. **Restrict Content Pro:** Designed primarily for content restriction and tiered access, ideal for protecting valuable digital assets like ebooks or video courses.

E. **Ultimate Member:** Focuses on creating vibrant online communities with user profiles, forums, private messaging, and social features.

F. **WP-Members:** A free and straightforward plugin for basic membership functionality, great for testing the waters before committing to a paid solution.

WordPress Considerations:

While offering vast flexibility and plugin options, WordPress (wordpress.org - NOT - wordpress.com) requires more technical knowledge for self-hosting.

Security and maintenance can be more demanding with self-hosted WordPress, but there are plugins for that too!

Other Platform Considerations:

Platforms like Wix, Squarespace, and Kajabi offer a user-friendly, all-in-one solution, but may have limitations on customization and scalability.

These platforms may also have higher monthly fees and less control over data migration.

Before you set sail on your digital adventure, choosing the right tech setup is crucial. To help you decide between WordPress and other platforms, consider these questions:

Functionality and Features:

1. What core functionalities do you need for your site? (Blogging, e-commerce, online courses, videos, forums, etc.)

2. Do you want to customize the platform's branding?

3. Do you want to customize the platform's features to your specific needs?

4. Does the platform offer built-in features for your desired functionalities, or will you need plugins?

Scalability and Growth:

5. Do you expect your site to grow in traffic and complexity over time?

6. Can the platform handle increased traffic and data storage needs?

7. Is it easy to upgrade and expand the platform as your site grows?

8. Are there limitations on features or plugins for higher-tier plans?

Technology and User Experience:

9. Are you comfortable working with self-hosted platforms like WordPress, or do you prefer a hosted solution?

10. How user-friendly is the platform interface for both you and your members?

11. Is the platform mobile-friendly and responsive across different devices?

12. Does the platform offer good security and performance optimization features?

13. At what stage do you need advanced development capabilities to

<u>Budget</u> <u>and</u> <u>Resources:</u>

14. What is your budget for hosting, plugins, themes, and other costs?

15. Do you need to hire people to help setup the site on a self-hosted platform?

16. Will you need to hire developers or designers to customize the platform?

17. How cost-effective is the platform in the long run?

18. Does the platform allow for your membership pricing model?

<u>Community</u> <u>and</u> <u>Support:</u>

19. Does the platform have a large and active community for support and troubleshooting?

20. Are there readily available resources and documentation for the platform?

21. Does the platform offer dedicated customer support, and if so, what level?

From Side-Hustle to Freedom Empire: Checklist for Building Your Membership Website Long Term Checklist

Building a successful membership site takes time, effort, and dedication. This checklist is a starting point, and you may need to adjust it based on your specific goals and audience. But with dedication and this roadmap in hand, you can set sail on your journey to building a thriving online community and achieving your dream of passive income and freedom from the 9-5 grind.

Foundational Steps:

- Define your niche and target audience: Who are you helping? What problem do you solve?
- Choose a membership platform: Consider features, pricing, and scalability.
- Plan your content strategy: What types of content will you offer? How often will you post?
- Set your pricing model: Consider tiered memberships, discounts, and promotions.
- Design your website: Make it visually appealing and user-friendly.
- Establish payment processing: Choose a secure and reliable system.

Building Your Community:

- Create a launch plan: Generate buzz and attract early members.
- Set up a welcome sequence: Onboard new members and explain the value proposition.
- Foster engagement: Encourage interaction through forums, comments, and live events.

- ✧ Gather feedback: Learn what your members want and adjust your offerings accordingly.
- ✧ Build relationships: Connect with your audience on a personal level.

Content and Value Creation:

- ✧ Diversify your content: Offer written content, videos, podcasts, webinars, etc.
- ✧ Deliver high-quality content: Provide valuable information that solves your audience's problems.
- ✧ Focus on consistency: Publish content regularly to keep your members engaged.
- ✧ Offer exclusive content: Give members access to special resources and behind-the-scenes insights.
- ✧ Partner with other experts: Collaborate to offer unique value and expand your reach.

Growth and Marketing:

- ✧ Optimize your website for SEO: Drive organic traffic and attract new members.
- ✧ Utilize social media: Promote your site and connect with potential members.
- ✧ Run targeted ads: Reach your ideal audience and drive sign-ups.
- ✧ Offer referral programs: incentivize existing members to spread the word.
- ✧ Track your results: Analyze data to see what's working and what's not.

Sustainability and Future-proofing:

✧ Automate as much as possible: Free up your time for more strategic tasks.

✧ Invest in tools and systems: Streamline your workflow and improve efficiency.

✧ Build a team: Delegate tasks and leverage expertise as your site grows.

✧ Continuously adapt and evolve: Stay up-to-date with industry trends and member needs.

✧ Never stop learning: Seek out new skills and knowledge to improve your site.

Pirate of Progress Reminders

Aye, matey! There are always hidden reefs and buried treasure in the membership site seas. Keep these advanced tips in your arsenal, captain, your membership site can sail smoother seas, discover hidden treasures, and build a thriving community of loyal crewmates!

Monetization Beyond Dues:

- Offer exclusive services: Consulting, coaching, one-on-one sessions for dedicated members.

- Leverage partnerships: Partner with other experts for joint webinars, courses, or product bundles.

- Host live events: Paid workshops, retreats, or conferences for deeper engagement and premium experiences.

- Create digital products: Ebooks, templates, checklists, or downloadable resources relevant to your niche.

Community Alchemy:

- Cultivate micro-communities: Break down your audience into smaller groups based on interests or levels for deeper connections.

- Empower superfans: Recognize and reward your most active members with badges, early access, or exclusive content.

- Host member spotlights: Showcase member achievements, stories, and expertise to inspire and foster collaboration.

- Run gamification campaigns: Encourage engagement with points, challenges, and leaderboards to boost activity and participation.

Content is King (and Queen!):

✧ Repurpose and repackage: Turn webinars into blog posts, podcasts into video snippets, and old content into fresh formats.

✧ Offer interactive experiences: Quizzes, polls, live Q&A sessions, and interactive courses to keep members engaged.

✧ Tap into member expertise: Host guest posts, interviews, or live sessions featuring talented members.

✧ Embrace user-generated content: Encourage members to share their experiences, tips, and insights.

Growth and Retention Hacks:

✧ Leverage referral programs: incentivize existing members to bring in new recruits.

✧ Run limited-time discounts and promotions: Create a sense of urgency and attract new members.

✧ Offer freemium memberships: Provide limited access to entice potential members and showcase your value.

✧ Personalize the onboarding experience: Welcome new members warmly, guide them through features, and answer their questions promptly.

✧ Conduct exit interviews: Understand why members leave and implement improvements to reduce churn.

Track, Pivot, Grow:

✧ Track key metrics like engagement, retention, and revenue to understand what works and what needs adjustment.

✧ Don't be afraid to try new things, analyze results, and adapt your strategies for continuous improvement.

✧ Never stop learning, exploring new tools and trends, and evolving your membership site to stay ahead of the curve.

Tech Stack Examples

Simple Membership Site with a Video Course and Forum

For a simple video course and forum membership site, both WordPress and Teachable have their merits. Choosing depends on your comfort with technology, budget, and future growth plans.

WordPress: Ideal if you prefer cost-effectiveness, customization, and full control over your site. Plugins like LearnDash, bbPress, and MemberPress offer powerful features for your needs.

Teachable: Perfect for beginners who want an all-in-one solution with ease of use and built-in features. Ideal for smaller communities or if you prioritize convenience over customization.

WordPress Setup:

Plugins:

- ✧ LearnDash: Powerful LMS plugin with drip feed functionality, quizzes, assignments, and certificates.
- ✧ bbPress: Popular forum plugin for building a vibrant community within your site.
- ✧ MemberPress: Secure and robust membership plugin for content restriction, tiered memberships, and payment gateways.

Benefits:

- ✧ Cost-effective: Plugins are affordable, especially compared to some dedicated platforms.
- ✧ Customization: WordPress offers vast flexibility for design and functionalities.
- ✧ Control: You own your data and platform, unlike with hosted solutions.

Drawbacks:

- ✧ Technical Setup: Requires some learning curve for managing plugins and WordPress itself.
- ✧ Security: Maintaining security updates and backups is your responsibility.
- ✧ Scalability: Can become complex for large communities or feature-heavy sites.

<u>Teachable</u> <u>Comparison:</u>

Benefits:

- ✧ Ease of Use: User-friendly interface for creating and managing courses and memberships.
- ✧ All-in-One: Built-in features for hosting videos, forums, email marketing, and payments.
- ✧ Scalability: Handles large communities and complex memberships effortlessly.

Drawbacks:

- ✧ Cost: Higher monthly fees compared to plugins, can become expensive as your site grows.

✧ Limited Customization: Less control over design and functionality compared to WordPress.

✧ Vendor Lock-in: Your data and platform are hosted by Teachable, limiting portability.

Remember, this is just a basic outline. Consider your specific needs and goals before choosing the best platform and plugins for your membership site.

May your learning voyage be a treasure trove of knowledge and your online community a haven of engaged supporters!

Complex Membership Site with Multifaceted Treasures

If your vision for your site includes video, community, e-commerce for digital products, advanced coaching services, a public blog, and pay-for-access posts, then what should you do? A multifaceted membership site demands a robust platform and the right tools. Let's explore both WordPress and Kajabi as potential captains for your digital ocean voyage.

WordPress: Ideal for technically savvy users who prioritize cost-effectiveness, control, and customization. The combination of plugins mentioned above provides powerful features for all your needs.

Kajabi: Perfect for those who value ease of use, an all-in-one solution, and convenient scalability. Ideal for larger communities or if you prioritize simplicity over granular control.

<u>WordPress</u> <u>Setup:</u>

Plugins:

- ✧ LearnDash: Powerful LMS for video courses with drip feed, quizzes, assignments, and certificates.
- ✧ BuddyBoss: Feature-rich community platform with forums, groups, user profiles, and social features.
- ✧ WooCommerce: Leading e-commerce plugin for selling digital products and managing purchases.
- ✧ MemberPress: Secure membership functionality for content restriction, tiered memberships, and payment gateways.
- ✧ Restrict Content Pro: Granular control over content access for pay-per-access blog posts.

✧ WPForms: Versatile form builder for creating applications and coaching intake forms.

Benefits:

✧ Cost-effective: Plugins are generally more affordable than Kajabi's monthly subscription.
✧ Flexibility and Control: You own your data and platform, and enjoy vast customization options.
✧ Scalability: Can handle large communities and complex features with proper configuration.

Drawbacks:

✧ Technical Setup: Requires knowledge of WordPress and plugin management, with a steeper learning curve.
✧ Security and Maintenance: Ongoing updates and backups are your responsibility.
✧ Integration Complexity: Coordinating multiple plugins can be demanding.

<u>Kajabi</u> <u>Comparison:</u>

Benefits:

✧ All-in-One Solution: Built-in features for courses, communities, e-commerce, landing pages, email marketing, and payments.
✧ Ease of Use: User-friendly interface simplifies site creation and management.
✧ Scalability: Handles large communities and complex features seamlessly.

Drawbacks:

- ✧ Cost: Monthly subscription can be expensive, especially for smaller sites.
- ✧ Limited Customization: Less control over design and functionality compared to WordPress.
- ✧ Vendor Lock-in: Your data and platform are hosted by Kajabi, limiting portability.

Bonus Tip: Consider hybrid solutions. You could host your public blog on WordPress and integrate it with Kajabi for your membership features, leveraging the strengths of both platforms.

Remember, this is just a roadmap. Dig deeper into your specific needs and resources before choosing the path that leads to your ideal membership site paradise. May your digital seas be bountiful and your community a loyal and thriving crew!

About the Authors

WordPress Experts
Membership Architects | Building Digital Empires Brick by Brick

For over a decade, we've been the secret weapon behind dozens of thriving membership empires across the globe. We're not just tech whizzes but are membership strategists who help passionate creators, and entrepreneurs chart their course to recurring revenue and community-fueled success.

Go forth and transform your passion into a recurring revenue stream.

"The best time to plant a tree was 20 years ago. The second best time is now."
- Chinese Proverb